CREATING
RELEVANT
RITUALS

Dr. Chris Harris is Principal Lecturer in religious education and Head of the Division of Arts, Australian Catholic University, Queensland. He has degrees in literature, theology, and religious studies and has taught on both the primary and secondary levels.

CREATING
RELEVANT
Rituals

▸ *Celebrations*
for Religious
Education

◂ **CHRIS HARRIS** ▸

E.J. DWYER

First published in 1992 by
E.J. Dwyer (Australia) Pty Ltd
3/32-72 Alice Street
Newtown NSW 2042
Australia

National Library of Australia
Cataloguing-in-Publication data

Harris, Chris (Christian), 1934–
    Creating relevant rituals : celebrations for religious education.

    Bibliography.
    Includes index.
    ISBN 0 85574 420 0.

    1. Ritual. 2. Religious education. 3. Rites and ceremonies. I. Title.

264

Distributed in Canada by:
  Meakin and Associates
  Unit 17
  81 Auriga Drive
  NEPEAN, ONT K2E 7Y5
  Ph: (613) 226 4381

Distributed in Ireland and the U.K. by:
  Columba Book Service
  93 The Rise
  Mount Merrion
  BLACKROCK CO. DUBLIN
  Ph: (01) 283 2954

Distributed in the United States by:
  Morehouse Publishing
  871 Ethan Allen Highway
  RIDGEFIELD CT 06877
  Ph: (203) 431 3927

Typeset in Palatino 11/13½ pt by Egan-Reid Ltd, Auckland, NZ
Printed in Singapore by Kim Hup Lee Printing Co Pte Limited

FOREWORD

Reading this book is an exercise in recovering a sense of the transforming power of human activity. The author, Chris Harris, shows that good ritual has the power to deliver both sides of religious experience—immanence and transcendence. Good ritual convinces the participants that God's presence is available (immanence) and inexhaustible (transcendence). Yet, those of us who work in religious education have long known that many Christians express their discomfort of a church which continues to be alienated from bodily existence. While liturgists have come to a deeper awareness of how the liturgy shapes the congregation, they are also quick to admit that people still are not comfortable with much of the liturgical reform of the last quarter century. Often people react to the implicit denial of their full humanity by withdrawing from the assembly. The systemic relation of these understandings of ritual to the role of the imagination is clear. It reflects in action what theology mirrors in its language, namely, that overly abstract theory separates what we believe in our hearts from what we claim with our lips.

No one knows this better than does the religious educator. But what to do about it? As one who has worked long in the field, Chris Harris sets out to show how ritual is formed and informed by the aesthetic dimensions of human experience, and how imagination is related to the promotion of appropriate and adequate rituals to express the significance of religious experience for Christians today.

The book is filled with concrete examples which illustrate the points that Harris makes and which help the text come alive. Religious educators will be able to identify with most of the situations he describes. He combines his own practical experience as husband, father, and parishioner with his professional role of teacher, writer, and thinker, to make the most salient of his points for religious education. First, he insists that religious rituals must use symbols that are rich in sensory power or else they become boring and are lost on people. Second, he shows that because all ritual is not liturgy, all religious educators must learn to use ritual as a regular part of religious education. They must become more confident and skilled in planning non-liturgical rituals.

But it is Harris's distillation of Victor Turner's notion of anti-structure and structure which is the most cogent section of the book. He helps the reader to realize that the anti-structure is the place of freedom to imagine. It is here that symbol and story are born. Structures yield sign and systems. It is in the anti-structure that feeling and intuition are cherished for what they yield, whereas it is in the structure that common sense and thinking are valued. The author takes great care to avoid the trap of dualistic thinking by his insistence that the religious educator must remember that human beings are liminal beings, that is, we are people who must live between the anti-structure and structure.

Today we recognize that we have been too stuck in the univocality of the structure. Here Harris shares with other writers the insight that participation in anti-structural reality is like a journey which moves out and back, or away and in return. This journey is much more than what Turner described as "spontaneous communitas" (the momentary interpersonal encounter). Nor does it connote an escape from culture, but rather it implies a journey of withdrawal for a time to deepen, broaden, and sharpen perspective.

Such an understanding gives more meaning and purpose to the term "retreat." That those of us who live in such a fast-paced technological world need retreat more than ever is evident from Harris's presentation in this book.

Although Chris Harris suggests that he is especially aiming at beginners, anyone interested in religious education can benefit from his efforts to help readers better understand and appreciate their own power and potential to enhance the religious lives of the people they serve through the fashioning of meaningful rituals.

This book deserves a wide and careful reading; once read, it is sure to elicit a thoughtful and immediate response.

Gloria Durka
Fordham University

ACKNOWLEDGMENTS

The author gratefully achnowledges the use of material from the following works. Every effort has been made to locate the sources of quoted material and to obtain authority for its use.

Religious Education Development, Gabriel Moran, Minneapolis, Winston Press & New York, HarperCollins Publishers, 1983.

Ritual in Industrial Society, R. J. Bocock, London, Allen and Unwin & Andover, Routledge, 1974.

"Confessions of a Practicing Catholic," Thomas Geoghegan, *America*, 158/13 (April 2, 1988).

"The Savior as Woman," Nancy K. Hill, *Cross Currents*, xxxix/1 Spring, 1989).

The Mass, J. Jungman, trans. J. Fernandes, Collegeville, The Liturgical Press, 1975.

"Ritual, Tribal and Catholic," V. Turner, *Worship*, 50/6 (November, 1976).

"Self-Generated Ritual: Trend or Fad?" V. Hine, *Worship*, 55 (1981).

The Worship of the Early Church, Ferdinand Hahn, copyright © 1973, Fortress Press. Used by permission of Augsburg Fortress.

The Ritual Process, V. Turner, Ithaca, N.Y., Cornell University Press, 1969.

The Idea of the Holy, R. Otto, tr. J. Harvey, New York, Galaxy, 1964. By permission of Oxford University Press.

"Unthematic Knowledge of God," in *Psychology and Religion*, ed. M. Gorman, New York, Paulist Press, 1985.

CONTENTS

INTRODUCTION   *xi*

CHAPTER ONE
▶ A Place for Ritual in Religious Education   1

CHAPTER TWO
▶ The Elements of Ritual—Symbol   15

CHAPTER THREE
▶ The Elements of Ritual—The Use of Symbols   31

CHAPTER FOUR
▶ The Elements of Ritual—Symbols Are Used
  to Express Meaning   39

CHAPTER FIVE
▶ Structure and Anti-structure—Applications   71

Conclusion   111

Recommended Reading   113

INDEX   114

CONTENTS

INTRODUCTION

This book is a product of a long developmental process. My absorption with ritual began during my doctoral studies at the University of Lancaster where I was first introduced to cultural anthropology. I found that other societies were not only fascinating in themselves but they also seemed to imply much about my own society.

The point was driven home to me during a conference on genetic engineering. I had presented a paper that argued against genetic determinism by stressing the variety of human behavior that clustered around the phenomenon of sexual attraction between men and women. My examples came from southern Africa, the Amazon basin, India and Spain. A later speaker also argued against genetic determinism with examples taken from central Europe. I was quite puzzled by his assumption that his European examples carried much more weight than my "exotic" ones.

I can see his point but continue to reject any assumption that our Western "civilized" societies are removed from the ways of less technologically developed societies. Anthropology has so much to tell us about the societies in which we live.

This conclusion led me to investigate the way rituals work not only in other societies, but also in my own. I have been helped by many colleagues and graduate students during my years at the McAuley campus of Australian Catholic University and my shorter stay at Fordham University, New York. These colleagues and students have worked with me in analyzing and developing rituals. Some of their work is acknowledged in the text of the book, but all of them have helped me in my exploration of ritual, and in the application of my discoveries to religious education.

CHRIS HARRIS

CHAPTER ONE

▸ *A Place for Ritual in Religious Education*

Approaches to "ritual"

"Ritual" is an unfortunate word. For many it denotes boring routine, or ceremony that has lost its soul and become "mere ritual." People involved in the practical enterprise of religious education may need to avoid the word. For them, a ritual may become a celebration, a happening, or something that is simply "done"... "Cathy's mother has died. What can we do when Cathy comes back to class?" Whatever words are used, it is fatal to associate religious education with what is boring or colorless. Still, the term, ritual, should not be tossed aside too hastily, as it has a precise use which religious educators need to explore.

Ritual is a phenomenon found in societies. It is part of culture, something produced by a society. Religion does not have a monopoly on ritual. There is a ritual dimension to religion, but not all ritual is religious. Great sporting events—the Olympic Games, Wimbledon, the Super Bowl, the World Cup—have strong elements of ritual, but are not demonstrably religious. The same can be said about political campaigns, rock concerts and the processes of law.

Social scientists have begun to explore the ways in which ritual functions in a society. Their findings have had some effect on writings by scholars with a religious point of view. Some of them have dealt directly with religious ritual. Victor Turner, particularly in articles in *Worship*, is one example. [1] Other writers have used the social sciences but maintain sacramental theology as their starting point; they begin with the sacraments and then reach out to secular disciplines to make further connections with the wider human context. Tad Guzie and Nathan Mitchell, for example, have consistently appealed to the broader human context in their work on sacraments. [2] The excellent *Alternative Futures for Worship*, under the general editorship of Bernard J. Lee, has used social scientists as members of its writing teams in presenting possible strategies for the development of sacramental worship.[3]

The approach in this book

I begin with the secular disciplines, particularly cultural anthropology, and then explore how anthropological findings can be used to clarify issues of sacramental theology.[4] The book is written to help practitioners and students of religious ritual to understand better the contribution of the social sciences to religious studies.

In particular, this book is written for beginners, people who have begun some serious study of religion or who feel drawn to begin. For such people, religion is a serious business. They tend to have a "religious mindset." Their view of the world is strongly affected by religion, and their work is or will be in the area of religious education. I take religious education in its widest possible context, as a way of reaching out to others to help them consider and experience possible ways of being in the world as religious persons.

Among religious educators, I include parents, teachers, priests, parish workers, counselors, spiritual directors, and students aspiring to join such professions. These people, at least, ought to be concerned with religious ritual and tend to approach it from a religious point of view. Most would admit that there are problems with religious ritual: the figures force the admission from all but the most optimistic. Even for the United States, which is above most Western countries in church attendance, the figures are not consoling.[5] But, despite these problems, they see religious ritual, especially liturgy, the official worship of the church, as a beneficial and vital part of life—its omission would be unthinkable.

I do not make this assumption. My own tradition is that of a Catholic Christian and my writing is bound to be shaped by it to a great extent, but I have tried to write from outside a religious mindset, setting out what some social scientists, particularly cultural anthropologists, have to say about ritual. This, I believe, can be of great assistance to religious educators. By studying how ritual functions in a society, they may be prevented from making unthinking assumptions about religious ritual. In recognizing the options open to ritual they may be better prepared for planning and analyzing religious ritual.

The approach taken in this book is, then, first to set out a body of anthropological theory and, second to apply this theory to the practice of religious education. Some basic questions will be asked. Why is ritual important? What is this particular ritual about? These questions will first be answered from the standpoint of cultural anthropology. There may be further debate from the standpoints of theology or scripture study. But the reader will know the broad human options that are open before calling on theological disciplines to help, or hinder.

Why is ritual important?

Why bother to work with ritual? Why is it so important? A theologian might begin with the existence of sacraments which are vital to the church's life. An anthropologist will begin by looking to the function of all ritual, including sacraments, in our society. For the cultural anthropologist it is important to think about ritual, to talk about ritual and to write about ritual because ritual pervades our whole society. Ours is often seen as a crass and materialistic society, impoverished in imagination and bereft of ritual. This is nonsense to an anthropologist. Our modern Western society is as obsessed with ritual as any other society. Western rituals have many functions, including material gain, but whatever the function, ritual is everywhere.

This is no surprise, for, without ritual, no society could survive. The anthropologist perceives that ritual is one of the chief instruments a society uses to express and pass on its values. This is ritual's most general function. One anthropological "definition" of ritual expresses it this way:

> ritual is part of a society's communication code for
> transmitting messages to one another about matters of
> ultimate concern and about those entities believed to have
> enunciated, clarified and mediated a culture's bonding
> axioms to its present members. [6]

Ritual and myth

Societies have many strategies for encoding important messages concerning the survival and expansion of their values, their "bonding axioms." Ritual is one such strategy—myth, or story, is another. Myth has received far more attention in religious scholarly circles than ritual. It deserves further mention here because ritual and myth often work together. The stories we heard as very young children contained values which we probably still hold. But these stories were told to us in ritual situations. We did not passively read them, unless we were very precocious readers. We were told the stories as part of the going-to-bed process where the story gained from the ritual of things shared between parent and child.

Myth is mentioned with ritual for a second reason. Both have enormous power because they are rooted in the imagination. A society expresses its values in its laws, its institutions and its ethical teachings. But ritual and myth not only state what is to be done or not done—they also reinforce their message by powerful appeals to the emotions and to the sensibilities. It is no wonder that they continue to pervade our society; they are too important to let die.

It could be argued that the twentieth century has done much to enhance this ubiquity of ritual and myth. It has become a truism that Western societies have become more pluralistic in this century. A plurality of competing value systems has been seen to replace the monolithic value systems of more traditional cultures. Myths and rituals once central to the entire society have tended to lose their wide appeal and have been adopted by smaller groups and coteries. But pluralism does not lessen the need for ritual and myth. If anything, it underscores their importance. Modern Western societies, far from being without ritual and myth, can be seen as battlegrounds where competing rituals and myths are struggling for power.

It would be wrong, though, to overemphasize this competitive element. Rituals and myths may battle for possession of the souls of people, but they do not appear to do so, because they are taken for granted, or, at least, their messages are. This is the source of their power. They carry us along because we are engaged emotionally in what is happening. We buy the message because disbelief is suspended.

Examples

Let's examine the process in two familiar, even traditional, ritual-myth situations.

1. GOLDILOCKS AND THE THREE BEARS

The first situation is that of parent telling child the story of Goldilocks and the three bears. There are many variations of this story in Western cultures, but English-speaking readers will remember the bears' refrain when they find that their house has been invaded: "Who's been sitting in my chair? Who's been sleeping in my bed? Who's been eating my porridge?" The theme is possessiveness. The child receives the message, supported with all the authority of parent speaking as one who cuddles and loves, that certain things are "mine", that it is okay to define self in terms of what is "mine", that possessions have a certain sanctity and that it is wrong of other people to use them. Without judging the rightness or wrongness of these messages, I am simply demonstrating that the ritual-myth situation can carry them.

A second ritual-myth situation carries messages which are quite contradictory to those of the Goldilocks story. It happens when young children hear the gospel account of Matthew 6:28 ff: think about the lilies of the field; they don't make any efforts to get things that make them look good; and yet... This story, related with the authority of a religion teacher or other significant adult, seems to tell the child that it is okay not to worry about owning things.

The amazing thing is that we seem to be able to carry these contradictory values along with us. We may consciously attempt to reconcile the two messages or we may allow one value and then the other to influence us by consciously dividing our lives into different compartments. Most of us are probably not even aware of these competing value systems. Life, in all its complexity, simply rolls on. We are shaped by values of which we are only dimly aware.

2. THE BARBEQUE

Another example of the value-carrying function of myth-ritual is found in the outdoor barbeque, as practiced in Australia. This time the ritual element is far stronger than the myth element.

Barbeques or cookouts have become popular in many Western countries, to a large extent replacing the "picnic." There are many similarities of practice across nations but there are also subtle differences of detail and emphasis, so I shall confine my analysis to the Australian barbeque.

I had taken the barbeque ritual for granted until I attended one where a Malaysian guest looked on in wonder and asked question after question. I began to realize that what Australians accepted as a familiar part of their communication code was quite mysterious to the stranger. Her questions forced me to analyze this familiar ritual and to articulate its messages.

The first thing that struck my Malaysian friend was that men did the cooking. Women sat and chatted while men lit the fire and cooked the meal. Meat was the principal item cooked and, indeed, was clearly regarded as the most important food in the ritual. Other food included salads which were beautifully prepared and required much more time and effort than the cooking of the meat. But, just as clearly, salads were secondary to meat in ritual importance. The salads had been prepared by women in home kitchens and brought outdoors to the barbeque.

The final ritual element worth mentioning is drinks. There was plenty to drink, both alcoholic and non-alcoholic. This was brought to the barbeque by all those attending. That is, although it is common for a host family to provide meat and salads, it is expected that guests will "bring their own" drinks. These drinks may be shared, but there is a strong expectation (and consequent sense of obligation) that guests will contribute to the liquid refreshment store.

Thus we have a complex segment of a communication code transmitting messages about matters of ultimate concern and about entities believed to enunciate, clarify and mediate the bonding axioms of the culture, to use the terms of anthropology. But what are these matters of ultimate concern? What are these entities expressing the bonding axioms of the culture?

One answer involves the myth of mateship, seminal to Australian society. This myth celebrates in many forms the identity of the "bushman," the Australian version of the frontiersman. In the nineteenth century Australian town-dwellers seemed merely distant facsimiles of their English counterparts. But the bushman, whether drover, prospector or shearer, was different. He developed a unique identity—a blend of physical toughness, courage in the face of hardship and fierce loyalty to his friends. Great emphasis was placed on this latter quality of mateship. One reason would seem the need for mutual support in a harsh environment. Perhaps another reason had to do with the bushman's almost invariable status as employee. Few bushmen owned their land. They worked for large land-owners and needed to support one another if they were to gain fair conditions of employment.

Even miners who "staked their claims" had to battle with officialdom. The early struggles associated with the miners' rebellion of the Eureka Stockade and the great strikes of the shearers' unions fed the myth of mateship. [7] This is a myth for men, and the bushman was precisely that—a man.

Women were minor characters in the great novels of male endurance. They waited at home, rarely accompanying their men into the bush. If they did come, they established homes and waited for their men's return from droving or shearing.

Of course, most Australian men are urbanites and always have been. From the beginning of European settlement in 1788, population has clustered in the coastal cities. But bankers, shopkeepers and teachers are not the stuff of myths, and bushmen are. For many Australian men the barbeque continues to transmit the bushman mateship myth. It is about something which Australian men consider to be of ultimate concern—the gathering of men. These men cluster around their fire, they provide for the dependent females. And they provide the bushman's staple food, meat.

Australian men are "mates." No such man sets himself up as master distributing largesse to his serfs. So each man is expected to contribute to the ritual feast by bringing something to drink. Women are participants in the ritual, but their major contribution, the salads, are considered to be of secondary importance. They often serve the salad, but the men serve the meat, either directly from the grate above the fire or by bringing it, with some ceremony, from the fire to the table for the women to distribute. The men clearly "provide" the cooked meat.

The "bonding axioms" of mateship and male dominance are

challenged in Australian society. Many women actively reject all that they include. But the ritual acts as a subtle purveyor of the mateship values. It has that taken-for-granted quality!

My wife is a fastidious cook who cannot bear to see how badly men sometimes prepare meat at a barbeque. I have known her to sidle perilously close to the group of cooking men to oversee what is going on. But not even she has been permitted to supervise the cooking of the meat! Her offers of help or advice have been politely but firmly refused.

Perhaps more subtle changes are already altering the ritual in other directions. Affluence, not mateship, may become the focus of celebration as more sophisticated gourmet foods replace steak and sausages as the principal food of the ritual. Such changes are likely, as the "bonding axioms" of one generation may not be those of another.

I suspect that other Western societies have similar complexes of meaning attached to outdoors activity. Is the American cookout linked to the myths of the old West? Does the British need to walk, to run or simply to be in the natural world hark back to Robin Hood or, perhaps, to the great British traditions of exploration? China, for all its crowdedness and lack of privacy, has its myth of the Taoist sage contemplating nature. This peaceful, lonely figure appears in many Chinese paintings. I leave readers to contemplate their own cultures and to make the links between ritual and myth.

You may think my analysis of the barbeque ritual is fanciful and that I am loading meaning onto a rather simple event. My response is that rituals are often simple events that are taken for granted. Consider another Australian mateship ritual where the same values are expressed but with quite a different set of actions:

Supposing a male friend of mine asks me to come to his house and help him lay a slab of concrete. This could be a big job so several of the man's mates gather. Intense physical work is serious business, and it is men's business. Women play a support role, so the "little woman" supplies tea and cakes or sandwiches at various breaks in the work. At the end of the job the host will probably provide a beer or two. None of the visiting men will bring food or beer. They are not expected to in this work ritual, because they are providing their labor, and the assumption is that they will be fed and watered for it. Further, they put the host male under an unstated obligation: he will be expected to help them when they ask him to join in their next work ritual.

This is clearly a "pay-back" system. Mates do not "bludge," to use the colloquial Australian term. Instead they fulfill their obligations to pull together. Again, simple rituals can carry quite complicated systems of values and demands.

Rituals, then, express and pass on values. New rituals are devised for new values and become popular as new values develop. But the ritual, with its taken-for-granted quality, has something of a conservative function; it tends to pass on what has "always" been held dear, what is obviously "to be done."

Implications for religious education

If anthropologists are right and ritual functions as a transmitter of messages about matters of ultimate concern, how should religious educators react? One general recommendation is that they pay greater attention to ritual. Story-telling has moved the theory of myth into the classroom. Adults, too, have been encouraged to "tell their story" as part of their religious growth. [8] Far too little attention has been paid to ritual in the past. Even in Catholic religious education, known for its stress on the sacramental, there has been a near universal habit of compartmentalizing ritual into formal celebration of one of the seven sacraments.

However, anything can be ritualized. Any value the educator wishes to pass on can be expressed in ritual. Any exploration of values, or bonding axioms, in a group can use ritual as an instrument. [9] Ritual, then, should be built into the religious education curriculum. It is too important to be treated as an optional extra. [10]

The events of the liturgical year are obvious foci for religious ritual. But other more secular events can also be ritualized in religious settings. Valentine's Day, Mother's Day, Father's Day and national holidays are examples.

More important is the need for religious educators to be on the lookout for chances to use ritual. The joy of being noticed on a birthday, the comfort when grief is shared—these are felt in rituals. It is important not to miss opportunities of doing something when we can—and "doing something" is ritual.

Sample Rituals

The first example focuses on children's very first day in primary school. The teacher involved was tired of the accepted wisdom that parents should be sent off home as quickly as possible on that possibly tear-filled first morning. She argued that one aim of her school was to unite children, parents, teachers and administrators in the educational process. Yet, on the first day, parents were being told to "go away." So she designed a simple set of rituals to give a very different message.

Parents were welcomed into the classroom with their children. They helped the children find lockers and coat hooks. Each parent or pair of parents introduced their child to the class. A very simple but affirming introduction was asked for. The teacher told the parents how happy she was to have their special children in this classroom that now belonged to all of them. She told how each child would prepare a "me box" with cut-out shapes of hands and feet, coloured string exactly as high as the child etc. These boxes would be presented to the parents when they returned to meet the children in the afternoon.

The tasks for the day were clear, and the simple ritual of showing parents the results of the tasks completed the school day. Basic ritual—easy to do—but important!

The second example is a ritual in which a family celebrated a daughter's reaching maturity. It, too, involved simple elements: the girl's acceptance of a photo of her parents and an expression of her love for them; the parents' statement of trust in their daughter and admiration for her. [11] Again, simple but important in our culture where there is no clear ritual of initiation into adulthood. For years parents insist, "You're not old enough to…," while the teenager is sure he or she is old enough to…

Analysis of ritual

Religious educators need to involve themselves in another task, that of analyzing ritual. The accepted rituals of a society carry values that members of the society should be aware of and question. The old dictum that the unexamined life is not worth leading applies to ritual.

The relative lack of importance attributed to "women's work" in the barbeque indicates a value, or lack of value, that needs questioning. The traditional wedding with its separation of groom's family and bride's family needs questioning. Do we really accept that marriage involves the transfer of a woman from one clan to another? Do we really accept that a father owns his daughter and, in marriage, "gives her away" to another man's ownership? Some members of Western societies will give an affirmative answer to both questions. Many will not. But the "traditional wedding" ritual implies an affirmative response.

Anthropology is not usually concerned with which answer is correct. It does ask that we be aware of what is going on in the ritual and what values the ritual carries. Religious education is also in the business of increasing awareness, and it may also go on to raise questions about the rightness and wrongness, the appropriateness or lack of appropriateness, of the values the aware person notes in ritual.

At this stage we need to explore further how ritual works in society. To do this more anthropological theory, in particular, an analysis of ritual into certain elements, will help.

Discussion Questions

1. What does the term, ritual, mean to you?
    —Your immediate, "off-the-top-of-your-head" response?
    —Your considered opinion?

2. What myth-ritual complexes do you notice in your culture? What values do these complexes (or any one of them) carry?

3. If ritual is important, what differences should this make in *your* religious education context, i.e., your classroom, your home, your parish …?

Notes
1. Turner, V., "Passages, Margins and Poverty: Religious Symbols of Communitas," *Worship,* Part I, 1972; 46(7): 390-412; Part II, *Worship,* 46(8): 482-94; "Ritual, Tribal and Catholic," *Worship,* 1976; 50(6): 504-26.
2. Guzie, T., *Jesus and the Eucharist,* New York: Paulist, 1974. Guzie, T., *The Book of Sacramental Basics,* New York: Paulist, 1981. For Nathan Mitchell, see his work in Mitchell, N. (ed.), *The Rite of Penance, Commentaries,* Vol. III: *Background and Directions,* Washington, D.C.: The Liturgical Conference, 1978.
3. Lee, Bernard J. (General Editor), *Alternative Futures for Worship,* 7 volumes, Collegeville, Minnesota: Liturgical Press, 1987.
4. Cf. Paul J. Philibert's use of psychological theorists, particularly Erikson, to raise questions about sacramental theology: "Readiness for Ritual; Psychological Aspects of Maturity in Christian Celebration," in Duffy, R. (ed.), *Alternative Futures for Worship,* Vol. I, 63-121.
5. See *Notre Dame Study of Catholic Parish Life,* Reports 4 and 6, both edited by David C. Leege and Joseph Gremillion (1985).
6. Turner, V., "Ritual, Tribal and Catholic," *Worship,* 1976, 50(6): 504-26, in particular pp. 504-5.
7. Ward, R., *The Australian Legend,* Melbourne: O.U.P., 1966.
8. Shea, J., "Storytelling and Religious Identity," *Chicago Studies,* 21/1 (Spring 1982), 23-43.
9. Nadel, S.F., *Nupe Religion,* London: Routledge and Kegan Paul, 1954, p.99.
10. See Mary K. Oosdyke, "Acquiring a Sense of Liturgy in Contemporary Times," *Religious Education,* 84/3 (Summer, 1989), 323-37.
11. Expanded in Glenda Morgan's article, "Adolescent Ritual," *Liturgy News,* 17/4 (Oct.-Dec. 1987), 104-115.

CHAPTER TWO

▸ *The Elements of Ritual –*
Symbol

Ritual—a whole!

It is difficult to define any term as complex as "ritual." It may be that we need to stop trying to find one essential element in the term. Perhaps it will be better to use Wittgenstein's notion that complex concepts are like threads; they are formed by twisting fiber on fiber, and "the strength of the thread does not reside in the fact that some one fiber runs through its whole length, but in the overlapping of many fibers." [1] As thread loses its strength if separated into its constituent fibers, the term "ritual" will lose its richness if we treat it as a series of discrete elements. More important, real rituals will be destroyed for us if we treat them as objects to be dissected or analyzed.

There is no one element running through the whole length of the term, "ritual." Instead, several elements belong to the term, but the emphasis on any one of these elements will vary from ritual to ritual.

Robert Bocock has made a brave attempt to explain ritual. He sees it as "… the symbolic use of bodily movement and gesture in a social situation to express and articulate meaning." [2] I feel that Bocock is right to stress "symbol" and "meaning," but his notion of symbol seems too narrow. He is concerned with emphasizing action, but items other than "bodily movement and gesture" can be symbolic. However Bocock comes up with a framework of elements which we can use. Rituals involve *symbols which are used to express and articulate meaning*.

I remember the artist, Colin Lanceley, explaining his liking for collage and commenting that ritual is a form of collage. This is another analogy which may help to explain how the basic constituents of ritual are related. The elements of ritual are like the layers or surfaces of a collage; you can put them together or break them apart, but the constituents do not equal the whole. Only the finished work has a sense of unity and an aesthetic impact. Ritual is always in danger if one part of it is stressed instead of the whole. We all remember religious services which were not good ritual because the sermon went on for too long, or the choir saw the service as a music recital.

Certainly good ritual is often untidy, even incoherent. It touches deep springs of human experience which are beyond neat formulation. But its impact is that of a living, though perhaps confused, organic whole—not that of a neat display of dissected parts.

Symbol as an element of ritual

One distinction often made is that between a symbol and a sign. A sign is seen as giving a clear, unambiguous message. So a red traffic light means STOP. There is a clear correspondence between sign and message. Drivers are not usually given to writing sonnets about the peculiar beauty of the colour of a red light. They simply stop. But symbols act in a far more complex way than this. They are packed with meaning and are anything but unambiguous. If the sign/symbol distinction is valuable for making only this point, it has served its purpose.

Sand, for example, is not usually thought of as a symbol. It simply exists without having too much meaning attached to it. But sand is highly symbolic for a friend of mine. She told me that she had visited the land of her ancestors, Latvia. She had managed to bring various objects through customs: a gold cross belonging to her grandmother, some old photos and some sand. I could understand that the cross and photos could carry great meaning for her and her family, but sand? Then she explained. When Latvians are buried their relatives throw soil or sand onto the coffin. In Latvia this is Latvian soil, of course. But for Latvians who now live outside their native land it is highly significant to have some Latvian soil or sand which can be thrown into their graves at their burial. Here, sand has acquired a great deal of meaning. It is no longer a simple object; it is a symbol.

Usually rituals have to do with objects "outside normal technological usage." In this sense, many objects are not symbolic; they are the tools of everyday use. But they may become symbols.

I remember a particular tool my father had. It was a steel hook with a wooden handle. He used it for moving such cargo as wool bales at his work on the wharves. One of my earliest childhood memories is of him slipping this hook into his belt before going off to work. After he retired the hook was stored away. My father died but it was not until almost twenty years later that my mother died and I found the hook while I was cleaning up the old home. I brought it to my own home and hung it in the living room.

One evening a year or so later, a good friend, a man who worked with his hands, noticed the hook and took it down and examined it. When I told him its story his face lit up with wonder. "Think of the years of toil that have shaped that handle," he said.

Reflect for a moment on the stages of the development of this symbol. When my father first bought the hook, it may have been just a tool. I suspect that even then, for him, it was "my hook." Remember the three bears—"Who's been sitting on *my* chair?"! For me, the object gathered more meaning and became encrusted with memories as my life progressed. My friend's comment about the handle articulated this and added more memories. Now, the hook reminds me of him, as well as of my father.

If you reflect on your own possessions you will probably find examples of this growth of symbolic significance. There may be pictures, postcards or ornaments which you treasure because of the meaning they have come to have for you. Of course, your treasures may be another person's junk. Symbols have to do with what Lost and Found columns call "sentimental value."

Public and private symbols interact

Many symbols are private; they carry meaning for one person, but not for another. They may be used in private rituals, but it is unlikely that they will figure on public occasions. My father's hook is a private symbol. It carries meaning for me and for close family and friends who know its significance. Sand from Latvia is a more public symbol. Its significance is known to a far wider circle, at least among the Latvian community.

It would be wrong, however, to place symbols in too tight a

private/public classification. Our private symbols are already affected by the culture in which we live. Certain objects are simply not used as private symbols in our culture and it is unlikely that an individual will go against the taboo. So, in some societies the shrunken skulls of ancestors are kept almost as we keep photos. European societies of a few centuries ago saw nothing gruesome in keeping bones from graveyards, and even arranging them in pleasing patterns. While today's tourist might stroll along the Via Veneto to see such things, he or she is not likely to go home and do likewise.

Good ritual demands that there be interplay between the two spheres, public and private. If public ritual does not touch my inner world it will become a boring duty that I, at best, endure.

Sample Ritual

This is taken from an unpublished ritual designed by Elizabeth Callaghan. Elizabeth's ritual was worked out for, and with, a family, one of whose sons was dying from AIDS. The son—let us call him Len—was weak, but still capable of coming home for a "last family meal." A ritual preceded the actual meal. In Elizabeth's words:

> The symbol chosen is a large wooden cross. For Len this symbol holds strength to endure suffering. It was decided that at some time during the ritual all would hold the cross, hand over hand. As each member places their hands over another's they will say something they have wanted to say to Len. It was also decided that all will write their names on the cross towards the end of the evening.

> Another decision was that the family will prepare the room into which Len is to enter; comfortable seating, candles and incense. His sister has chosen jasmin incense because that is what grew along the fence near their bedrooms when they were children. Len is to enter into their family circle of held hands. I think few words will be said, just holding and crying. Each in turn will embrace Len and welcome him. Len has also decided to bring gifts for his family. He has carefully chosen some of his personal items to give to each of his

family. Len's mother has brought along new clothes which he will change into during the evening. Bread and wine will form part of the meal.

Notice the mixture of public and private symbols used here. The cross has meanings shared by so many Christians. Yet, here, it may take on very special meanings for this family. As Elizabeth suggests, "for Len and his family, the cross may evoke feelings of shared suffering, a sense of solidarity and family or a sense of hope." The bread and wine of the meal are similar public symbols which carry eloquent meanings for this "last supper." The gifts which Len has chosen for members of his family are private symbols but probably carry meanings with which most people could identify. They certainly fit into the universal theme of the "significant gift."

Public symbols and social values

Public symbols are an anthropologist's concern. Bocock is right to stress the "social situation" of ritual. Ritual, after all, is a vehicle for the expression and passing on of a society's values. It performs this function when it appeals to large numbers within a society. It is possible to argue that ritual symbols can carry values very efficiently.

It seems, at first, a contradiction to speak of symbols as efficient. They are so rich, so diffuse, so imprecise. If you try giving objects symbolic value, this soon becomes obvious. Suppose you are in a group where you are asked to choose some object to symbolize how you feel at this moment. You may choose a rock, flower or a silver coin. You know what you are trying to express. To you, the rock may symbolize strength and solidity; the flower, joy; the coin, value. But others in the group need your explanation. It is quite easy for them to give interpretations that are the reverse of your positive values. To them, the rock may represent hardness, coldness; the flower, fragility; and the coin, "filthy lucre" or betrayal (selling Jesus for thirty pieces of silver).

I remember my own response to the ritual Elizabeth Callaghan worked on with Len and his family. My first reaction was that the wooden cross could only signify sorrow. Elizabeth's suggestion that it could speak of hope did not ring true for me. Now I have changed my mind. The probable cause of my change was Petrea King's book, *Quest for Life* [3]. Petrea works with people who have life-threatening diseases, AIDS and cancer. She refuses to call those diseases terminal. Her optimism is enormous. For her, Christ is a source of positive strength. Because of her I can see that the cross can mean sorrow, and also hope, joy and glory.

Symbols are multivalent

This multivalence seems to belong to the very nature of symbols. The English word, symbol, is derived from Greek words which denote a bringing or throwing together. Two rivers could come together at a junction, shields could be locked together, people could come together at a meal, two stories could be brought together and compared, things could come together accidentally or as a coincidence. Luke's gospel uses the word for Mary's pondering, mulling over the strange words of Simeon and Anna in the Temple (2:19). The Greek has much of the notion of collage. Things come together by accident; layer upon layer of meaning sits in our minds, and we try to sort them out. "Symbol" denotes rich confusion.

Other languages have something of this meaning, too. The Ndembu people of Zambia see ritual symbols as blaze-marks which help them to move from the known to the unknown and back again. They serve a purpose analogous to "… cutting marks on a tree with one's axe or … breaking and bending branches to serve as guides back from the unknown bush to known paths. The symbol, then, is a blaze or landmark, something that connects the unknown with the known." [4]

The Desana of the Amazon basin live along the upper reaches of the Vaupes River. Their world is dominated by the sounds of running water. They turn to hearing for a concept of "symbol." For them, a symbol has "echoes." It has a quality of mysterious sound. One needs to listen carefully to it to pick up even some of the hidden qualities of this sound. [5]

Our term, "symbol," deals with the not-immediately-known. The symbolic is not clear or logical. It denotes multiplicity of meaning. It usually appeals to our minds, emotions, desires and to our feelings. Yet, despite this complexity, the symbol can be seen as a very efficient carrier of social values. In his early work, Victor Turner argued that symbols are efficient precisely because of their complexity.

Turner noted that among the complex of symbols in a ritual one usually stood out. This was the "dominant" symbol. The cross would be the dominant symbol in Len's ritual. The chief properties of such dominant ritual symbols are condensation, unification of disparate significata and polarization of meaning. I have already dealt with the first two of these properties: symbols are packed with meanings and these meanings can be disparate, even contradictory.

The two poles of a symbol

The third property needs further explanation. Polarization of meaning refers to the grouping of a symbol's meanings around one or another of two "poles": a sensory pole and an ideological pole. The meanings or significata of ritual symbols tend to group around either the sensory or the ideological pole. Sometimes "physiological" or "orectic" are used for sensory. This pole gathers meanings rich in sense data and/or emotional data. The ideological pole gathers meanings relating to more abstract ideals.

A further example of ritual symbols in Western cultures would be the engagement and wedding rings most married women wear. My wife wears a diamond engagement ring which we bought in Cairo. Her wedding ring is the gold band which my mother wore as her wedding ring. These ritual symbols carry many meanings for us. At the sensory pole cluster meanings of appearance (the rings look good), of romance (memories of far off, exotic places) and of emotion (memories of dead loved ones). At the ideological pole cluster meanings of duty (marriage promises) and of social bonding.

Turner argues that the two poles interact, so that the duty elements of the ideological are made to seem desirable because of the sensory elements, and the sensory elements are ennobled because of the ideological. Thus the rings are symbols in a ritual complex which is designed to make duty seem highly desirable.

And the rings are not merely pretty baubles but are given dignity and value because of the obligations they represent. Ritual is, then, a "mechanism" which "converts the obligatory into the desirable." [6]

This is even clearer if we examine the whole ritual of marriage. The marriage service usually spells out a series of heavy obligations: lifelong fidelity between the spouses, care of children etc. In the past it has been seen as essential to society's continuation that such obligations be honoured. Even recent "permissive" elements in Western societies seem to have kept the obligations as an ideal. Daunting duties cluster at the ideological pole.

The sensory significata assure the couple that accepting these duties is not only a good thing, but an enjoyable one. The couple usually dress in some form of "finery," they gather with friends and family at some form of "feast," and they are given gifts. Perhaps more importantly they are congratulated; they are told many "good" things. That is, no matter what people's private misgivings are, they tend to assure the couple that they will be happy, that all will be well for ever more and that now they look the picture of happiness and beauty and/or handsomeness.

All this acts to convert the obligatory into the desirable. It is intended that this happen not only for the couple, but also for all present at the wedding. The ideal of happy marriage is put before the unmarried, and the married are reminded of the obligations they joyfully accepted in the past. The social situation of the ritual gives it a power of expressing and promulgating the values of "happy marriage." The repetition of such rituals throughout society and from generation to generation is intended to make these values "permanent." The ritual enunciates, clarifies and mediates the bonding axioms of our society.

The very complexity of ritual symbols contributes to their efficiency in passing on values. Because symbols refer to both sensory and ideological qualities, norms and values, on the one hand, become saturated with emotion, while the gross and basic emotions become ennobled through contact with social values. The irksomeness of moral constraint is transformed into "love of virtue." [7] All this happens within the context of actual ritual. The almost limitless scope of a symbol's meaning is directed, within a context, to certain ends.

You could object that this emphasis on polarization of meaning converts ritual into a gigantic confidence trick. To change the metaphor, ritual coats the bitter pill of duty with a sweet coating of desirability.

This has certainly happened in the past. Think of the propaganda rituals of parades and rallies that have convinced men they were marching off to glorious war when the most mercenary of motives were the cause of such wars.

But surely rituals are more than mechanisms which ensure conformity to what society expects! Turner agreed later that they are, but his impatience with the view that "...rituals were designed as some sort of all-purpose social glue" [8] is something which grew. The early Turner was inclined to accept the standard anthropological view, derived from Emile Durkheim and still very much alive, that rituals exist to ensure that we fulfill social requirements.

Implications for religious education

Of course there is more to ritual than making us accept social, and religious, duties cheerfully. But this is one of its functions, and ritual can perform this function efficiently because it uses symbols that are rich in both sensory and ideological meanings. This is important because it has great relevance to religious education. Religious rituals lose most of their impact on people when the symbols used lack sensory power. And this is happening! Religious rituals are not desirable; to many they are boring.

Liturgists have become far too ethereal in their attitude to religious symbols. The wafers used at Mass do not look like or taste like bread. The cup, rarely shared by the laity, holds wine that lacks richness and redness. The water of baptism is hardly seen by the onlookers. The odor of the chrism of confirmation is seldom picked up outside the sanctuary. From an anthropological point of view, religious symbols are "wee and timorous beasties," to use the words of Robert Burns.

The idea of a dominant symbol has been lost. Of course, it is common knowledge that bread and wine are the dominant symbols of eucharist, and that water is the dominant symbol of baptism.

Our theology says this; our ritual words say it. But we whisper it almost inaudibly in the language of sight and action. Perhaps it is time to bring back an offertory procession in which bread and wine are brought forward in recognizable form, as loaves and bottles, and laid on or near the altar. The dominant symbols must dominate.

I remember visiting a newly completed French church in which the baptismal font had water trickling into it continuously. The pastor who had inherited the church which someone else planned was critical of the symbol. This trickle disturbed people during Mass! It sounded like a "child peeing," to quote the priest. As a dominant symbol it was a failure.

A Jesuit friend told me of arguments in Zimbabwe: the people wanted baptism in the local river (where water was clearly a dominant symbol which dominated!), while the official rubrics required that the sacrament take place in a church.

Many religious educators have been hurt by taking sides in such arguments. They feel that, in their particular situation, they can do little to change sacramental ritual. This may be so, but there is a more widespread problem that all religious educators can help to overcome: the separation of the religious from the sensory. It occurs when folk become so holy and so goody-goody that they ignore the obvious human elements of ritual.

Infant baptism can be used as an example. I have asked groups of adult students to map out the sensory and ideological poles of this ritual. At the sensory pole they place water, oil and candle but they tend to miss what is important to the participants: the family gathering, the gifts, the baptismal robe passed on from one generation to another. These latter elements may be peripheral to the sacrament, though the baptismal robe, symbolizing the new life in Christ, is certainly central even to the sacrament. But each of these elements can be seen as central because each points to the child's acceptance into a family which is, for most children, the way into the church. Yet it is common for the official "religious" people at the ritual to ignore these family elements.

Religion seems to focus on water, oil and candle. Most people do not understand what these are about, and they are used in so niggardly a fashion that they are scarcely noticed. Religion ignores the more obviously desirable elements of the ritual, the family celebration. It does so at its peril.

People, too, can be symbolic. For years a conversation starter was "Do you remember what you were doing when the news of J.F.K's assassination came through?" Even today the factual biographies have not quite destroyed the idealism the president symbolized. In family baptisms people take symbolic roles; they are chosen because they embody certain qualities.

The baptism of Daniel Joseph Ryan Hutton brought this home to me. The chief celebrants of the ritual were Daniel's parents, David and Tricia. In their welcome they stated their reasons for choosing Jill and Geoff, Damien and Cathy as Daniel's godparents, and their reasons for choosing Gary as the priest who would baptize Daniel. In another beautiful exchange Gary said: "Tricia and David, you have named your son Daniel Joseph Ryan. Tell us why you have chosen these names."

These simple touches allow the emphasis to shift from anonymous formality to the richness of human involvement. There is an articulation of what people and names mean to *this* family. We need more religious educators like Tricia and David, people who realise that the human must not be peripheral to the officially sacred.

Attention to symbol can be the starting-point for a far-reaching analysis of what theology is about. The Church's traditional symbols need new life breathed into them.

Sometimes this is a matter of resurrecting ancient meanings that have been buried under layers of very doubtful theology. So, the symbolism of water in baptism needs to be explained in terms of such key scripture texts as Romans 6:1–4, where the stress is not on washing but on passing from death to life.

At other times the analysis of a traditional symbol can be startlingly new, as with Nancy Klenk Hill's understanding of the cross. [9] She begins her analysis with, "My thesis is simple: Jesus Christ died in childbirth." She goes on to argue that the cross is a symbol of passive suffering where Jesus bore pain in order to bring forth new life, just as "women enter pain and danger (when) they give life to a new generation of strangers." For Hill, the cross is not so much about "male" values, such as victory over evil or, as Augustine had it, the sexual act of the nuptial bed where Christ consummated his marriage with the Church. It is linked to the female values of the pains of childbirth, which lead to joy as John explicitly states (16:16–25, 29).

Some of the Church's ancient symbols have been forgotten, and can usefully be brought back to notice. The desert, the lonely place where a person meets God, is perhaps as central to Old Testament thinking as the Temple was. It was, too, a revered place for the eremetical tradition of many of the early fathers and mothers of the Church. It seems to me that the theme of desert appeals to many in our modern societies who need times of quiet so desperately. In Australia the desert, the outback, is a constant presence. Coast-dwellers go there sometimes. Perhaps more often they go to the beach or the sea or the bush. A basic drive for city folk in Australia, the Americas, Europe, even Hong Kong, seems to be to "get away from it all" if possible. We need to celebrate this spiritual quest, to encourage a going apart to quiet places whether these be actual physical locations or, more fundamentally important, the quiet places of the mind.

Religious educators can adopt an entirely different strategy in the use of symbols, to look for new symbols rather than traditional ones. This can be effective in liturgy but obviously is better suited to rituals which are designed outside the established frameworks. The quest is for new symbols, objects or persons which our twentieth century has loaded with meaning.

I think of Thomas Merton being inspired by Bob Dylan, whose records he often played in his hermitage days. [10] I think of the artist, Fred Cress, who uses images of the broken, the discarded... rubbish, broken glass... which speak of the throw-away society, capable of discarding people and so of soiling the planet. He also uses the screen (film, video, television) as the twentieth-century mask which hides us and yet magnifies our projections.

Besides symbol, there are other elements of ritual which need analysis. Although important, symbol is not the foundation element of ritual. If we look for symbols and build rituals around them, we often are wrong. It's like the story—apocryphal, I hope—of the teachers who were mightily impressed by smouldering gum tree logs and managed to get the massive things into the local church. Children, gathered for a prayer service, were very impressed by the glowing embers but were given no clue what the whole business was about. Symbols can mean many things; they must be given direction in ritual.

Discussion Questions

1. Name an object or person which means a great deal to you. Is this object or person a symbol?
   If so, in what ways? What meanings does the object or person carry for you?

2. What links can you make between public and private symbols?

3. Name a ritual which affected you deeply.
   What was the dominant symbol in the ritual?
   Do you find Turner's "two pole theory" useful for explaining how the symbol *worked*? Why?

Notes
1. Wittgenstein, Ludwig, *Philosophical Investigations*, translated G.E.M. Anscombe, Oxford: Blackwell, Part I, p.67.
2. Bocock, Robert, *Ritual in Industrial Society*, London: Allen and Unwin, 1974, p. 37.
3. King, Petrea, *Quest for Life*, Sydney: Equinox, 1988.
4. Turner, V., *The Forest of Symbols*, Ithaca, London: Cornell University Press, 1967, p.48.
5. Reichel-Dolmatoff, G., *Amazonian Cosmos*, University of Chicago Press, p. 94.
6. Turner, V., *The Forest of Symbols*, Ithaca, London: Cornell University Press, 1967, pp.27-30.
7. *Ibid.*, p.30.
8. Edith Turner's phrase: see Edith Turner (ed.), *On the Edge of the Bush*, Tucson: University of Arizona Press, 1985, p.3.
9. Hill, Nancy Klenk, "The Savior as Woman," *Cross Currents*, xxxix/1 (Spring, 1989), 1-9.
10. Burton, Christie D., "Rediscovering Love's World: Thomas Merton's Love Poems and the Language of Ecstasy," *Cross Currents*, xxxix/1 (Spring, 1989), 64-82.

CHAPTER THREE

▸ *The Elements
of Ritual –The
Use of Symbols*

Rituals involve action

Ritual requires that symbols be used; something must be done with the symbols. This action requires that living bodies move. Ritual action is bodily action, not passive action, such as contemplation.

Of course, symbols can be contemplated or thought about. This happens at every thoughtful reading of myth. And some symbols, such as flags, are often "just there." But, in ritual, something is done: the myth is acted out, the flag is saluted or burnt. Ritual involves corporeal activity.

Sometimes this activity takes the form of an action done with symbols. One can break consecrated bread and eat it. This is ritual. The presence of consecrated bread, the Real Presence, is not ritual per se. Something must be done with the bread.

Sometimes ritual activity is symbolic in itself. In our society there are ritual gestures of bowing, symbolic of submission or respect, of spitting, symbolic of contempt, or of standing ramrod straight, symbolic of attentive readiness. More precisely something is done with a symbol here, too, the symbol being the human body.

Indeed the human body is the primary symbol of ritual, the Ur-symbol. We move it to express meaning, we hold it still to express meaning. We clothe it in an endless variety of ways. We tattoo it, or mark it with scars. We clean it, or let it get dirty. We shave its head, or braid, comb or adorn this same hair. We open our mouths in loud laughter or keep them demurely closed. Some of these things we do almost without thought. But all of them are, in one society or another, highly symbolic actions that are integral parts of important rituals. [1]

The problem of passivity

Action is such an obvious constituent of ritual that we tend to take it for granted. Of course ritual is dynamic, not static. Of course ritual is dramatic, not merely narrative. But this active nature of ritual is a major problem in religious traditions where people have been pressured to attend rituals. These people have become passive spectators.

In a famous letter to the Mainz Liturgical Congress, Romano Guardini, one of the important figures in the liturgical movement which influenced Vatican II thinking, drew attention to the passive nature of much Catholic ritual. He begins by commenting that liturgy was rare in nineteenth-century Catholicism. The stress, particularly at the eucharist, was on individual worship carried out in a ceremonial context. Liturgy, says Guardini, is not individual worship. It requires that people pray together. Further, it demands that *whole persons* pray actively together. Words are not really important; actions are. The community must be involved in walking up with the gifts, in the washing of hands. Even their watching must become "seeing," looking with attention because they are involved. The eucharist is an act: "the act is done by every individual, not as an isolated individual, but as a member of a body in which the Church is present." [2]

Guardini raises serious questions for religious educators. He wonders whether twentieth-century congregations are capable of liturgical action, so used to passivity have they become. There are some helpful trends, he notes. The stress on the whole person in education is one of these.

Guardini's pessimism should not be put aside lightly. It is an open question whether many Christian congregations are capable of liturgical action. The reason for this cannot be the general passivity of the members of these congregations; the same folk who sit dully in the pews are anything but dull at football games. The point is that in liturgy they have been taught to be passive. The lesson is reinforced every Sunday by the architecture of churches. The action takes place in the sanctuary, usually on a raised platform. The folk on the exit side of the sanctuary watch a performance by specialist liturgists. These "act" in full view of the passive audience.

Other expectations reinforce the lesson that the church is a place where worship is, for most, a quiet, passive thing. One is the taboo on interaction. The church is a holy place, a sacred space. In Catholicism it has long been the holy of holies where God is present in the Blessed Sacrament. The glory of the Shekinah requires awed worship. Again, the architecture is wrong. The Blessed Sacrament should be reserved for worship in a side chapel. The main body of the church building is for the assembly of the Christian community.

What can religious educators do?

Religious educators can raise awareness that a community should claim its celebration space for action. They can increase expectation that a congregation will be active. They can teach skills in activity. One ploy I have seen work is to assign some form of dramatization of the gospel to a variety of groups in the parish. For example, once during Lent the gospel would be dramatized by the adult catechumenate group preparing for baptism that Easter. At other times the parish youth group or the parish tennis club might be asked. Such groups need help to begin the process of pondering on what the gospel is about, and they need help to sharpen their presentation skills. Providing such help is work for religious educators. The point here is that such work needs to be done because it involves people in liturgy. Liturgy, like any other form of ritual, requires action as one of its basic constituents.

Liturgy is not the only human enterprise to be ossified into passivity. It seems that much of the education process is marked by passive acceptance. Students seem bored; they are being allowed to sit back and observe, with minimal engagement. Religious educators, indeed all educators, are called to challenge this state of the nation by promoting action. Blessed are those who organize fund-raising days for good causes, who welcome new parents and students in ritual and who farewell students in ritual.

Sometimes these celebrations are elaborate. I've seen such grand affairs on Ash Wednesday, where smouldering gum logs did come into their own! But the celebration can be very ordinary, as long as something is done.

Sample Ritual

One example of such a very ordinary ritual was organized by Kerrie Corcoran, a Brisbane high school teacher. The situation was familiar enough: a well-loved teacher was leaving the school where Kerrie also taught. In such situations it is very easy to do nothing, or to let the occasion pass with a few muttered, embarrassed good-byes from the students. But Kerrie planned a farewell with the final year art students (the departing teacher, Carolyn, worked in the Art Department). In Kerrie's words, this is what happened:

> The ritual was to be a surprise (as they knew Carolyn loved surprises.) The boys were to congregate at the beginning of lunch break in the Art Courtyard. Of course having it in this location was to bring a lot of curiosity from non-Art students. Carolyn was certainly surprised and overwhelmed by the occasion.
>
> Firstly a Year 12 boy gave her flowers, with of course a kiss. A Year 8 student then gave Carolyn a card from all the Art students; with some embarrassment he accepted a kiss from Carolyn. Next the "cup" was brought forward by a Year 11 student. It was very symbolic—it was a container that we used always in the Art room, a margarine container; here they felt this was appropriate. Carolyn drank from the container first, then passed it around to all the students.
>
> Next the food was brought out by the Year 9; Carolyn opened all the packets of chips, peanuts, and cheezals, sharing them among the individuals. The boys had shown much reserve until now, but like any group, the food and the drink caused a "party mood" to occur and soon there was laughter and noise as they shared the food. The cake was then brought by a Year 10 student; after saying a few short words Carolyn cut the cake and managed to give a small section to each student.
>
> This was then followed by a time in which much talk and

sharing occurred. Carolyn mixed with the boys exchanging hugs and kisses, and the odd photograph or two was taken.

The Lunch break was drawing to a close, most of the students had left, but there was still a handful of students who followed Carolyn into the classroom. What was strange was the unusual quietness in which they stood around. No more were they exchanging gossip, nor was there laughter. Replacing their usual expressions were these forlorn, bewildered expressions. They looked totally lost.

They simply stood there, waiting for Carolyn to say something, to talk to them. In Carolyn's casual way she said, "What's happening, guys?" They continued to stare at her. Not one of them uttered a word. Then one of them reached over and gave Carolyn a huge hug and I could see he was emotionally affected. This was all the others needed and soon the classroom was filled with noses being blown and handkerchiefs being used. Here were grown boys showing human emotions—it was great!!!!!!!

As I have said, the farewell ritual was not elaborate. It was packed with meaning and obviously touched deep emotions. It surprises me that our young people are touched by such rituals. Perhaps our society suppresses emotion so much that any release leads to a flood of feeling. But the point I want to make here is that the ritual happened. Something was done! There was action!

The educator in us probably makes us agree with Kerrie. It is great when grown boys show emotion. Perhaps, however, the release of emotion was not the primary purpose of the ritual. Rather, its chief purpose included the expression of deep affection for a much-loved person who was leaving the school. There is, perhaps, another element. Kerrie stresses this when she records Carolyn's last words as the boys moved off to class: "Don't forget me, remember me." It seems to me that Carolyn got it right. The ritual was about remembering, too. So the meaning of the ritual included farewell and remembrance, both focused on a special person. The ritual was about these, rather than being an educational strategy to make boys express emotion.

The meaning of ritual is a complex issue. In the next chapter I will explore it further, not by analyzing the possible meanings of endless rituals, but by setting out a framework which will help the planning and analysis of any ritual.

Discussion Questions

1. Do you think that the liturgies you attend are passive affairs for most who are there?
    If your answer is "no," what good things *are happening*?
    If your answer is "yes," what can be done to promote action?

2. What rituals have you organized?
    Were symbols used appropriately in these rituals?
    Was the pace of the ritual right?

Notes
1. See Polhemus, Ted (ed.), *Social Aspects of the Human Body*, Harmondsworth: Penguin, 1978.
2. "A letter from Romano Guardini," *Herder Correspondence*, Special Issue, 1968, 24-6. Guardini sent this letter to the Mainz Congress (April, 1964), which he was unable to attend in person.

CHAPTER FOUR

▸ *The Elements of Ritual – Symbols Are Used to Express Meaning*

Ritual as routine?

I have already dealt with ritual's function as a carrier of messages in a society. Rituals have meaning for those involved in them, and there is no area of meaning with which rituals cannot deal. Cultural anthropology sees ritual as one of the chief carriers of meaning in societies. From the point of view of this discipline, the stereotype of "dead ritual" or "mere ritual" is almost meaningless. Anthropology does not equate ritual and routine. This needs to be kept in mind, for, as I have already mentioned, many common sense uses of the word "ritual," do equate ritual and routine: "I go through a real ritual every morning: I get up, do my breathing exercises, begin breakfast with orange juice..." Often ritual becomes something dull or dead: "This year's graduation was just empty ritual." For an anthropologist "ritual" may refer to an oft-repeated ceremony or it may not. After all there is a first time for any ritual. More importantly, the term in anthropology does not carry the sense of deadly boring routine. It is possible that authorities will have enough influence to pressure people into performing rituals which have no meaning other than demonstrating the authorities' power. But this is relatively rare. For anthropologists, rituals express meaning, and lots of it.

This is not to say that ritual is never about routine. Brett Webb-Mitchell has researched the effect of rituals of routine on mentally handicapped members of one of Jean Vanier's l'Arche communities in London. [1] He found that such rituals as the set pattern of what was done at meals and coffee breaks gave these people security. The rituals seemed to help them make sense of their day, and to give meaning to their existence. Parents and teachers know how important the security of routine is for small children. We may all need the security, the "structure," which our getting-up and going-to-bed rituals, our meals and our patterns of commuting give us. But ritual can be more than routine and should not be equated with it.

An approach to meaning in ritual

The approach used will give a method for analyzing ritual rather than explaining the detailed meaning of any one ritual. This method will help planners decide what a particular ritual could or should be about. To explain the approach we must delve into anthropological theory in order to find a useful tool for analysis and a framework for planners to use. Religious educators need both tool and framework.

The approach is one sketched out in some of Victor Turner's later writings. Turner became disenchanted with a view that saw ritual as a method of social control. He began to see society as more than "a system of social positions." [2] He even began to suspect that society, far from being a system at all, was a sort of optical illusion. It looks organized, and people in authority keep on telling us it is, but it is basically fluid and indeterminate. [3]

There are, then, other realities than system, and ritual may express them.

Arnold van Gennep's seminal book, *The Rites of Passage*, provided a way forward. [4] Van Gennep found that life could be mapped into a series of states. In most societies, the states of foetus, child, adult, authority (as spouse, parent, chief, priest), elder and ancestor are recognized. Within each state a person's life is defined in relatively clear terms. But the passage between states is marked by unusual rituals—the rites of passage.

N'Kanga, a rite of passage

Turner was familiar with such rites as practised by the Ndembu of central Africa. He found that ceremonies such as Nkang'a, a girl's puberty ritual, fitted perfectly into van Gennep's scheme. [5] The ritual marked the passage from one state, that of being girl, to another state, that of being woman. Van Gennep's three phases were present: separation, margin and aggregation.

At the separation phase the girl was removed from normal Ndembu society. She was carried to a place in the forest outside her village and positioned at the foot of a mudyi tree. This tree produces a white latex when cut. The mudyi tree is the dominant symbol of the rite of separation, indicating, at the physiological pole, mother's milk and breasts and, at the ideological pole, the values of the line of women a person is descended from (the matriliny), particularly as these values are perceived by Ndembu women.

There are clear ideological differences between men and women in Ndembu society. Both accept the principles of matriliny and, in one sense, the mudyi tree represents the values of the whole society, what boys and girls learn at their "mother's knee." But boys and girls are instructed quite differently at the rites of passage which induct them into manhood and womanhood respectively. Similar deep ideological differences between men and women may exist in Western societies, too, but the accepted fiction is that both genders share the same values. [6]

The "war of the sexes" is played out on the first morning of Nkang'a. The women of the village return from the mudyi tree where they have left the girl, lying on her left (feminine) side and covered with a blanket. They rouse the men from sleep as roughly as they can, and bring them out to the initiation site. The women dance around the girl who must lie without moving a muscle no matter how hot she becomes under her blanket. The women insult the men all morning. They chant bawdy songs questioning male sexual prowess. The men are excluded from the circle of dancing women.

There is a change at noon. The senior women lift the girl and turn her on to her right (masculine) side. Now the men are invited to join the circle of dancers. Among the Ndembu the war of sexes is never allowed to go too far. There is recognition that men and women must ultimately work together if the society is to survive. It is by no means axiomatic that the society will survive. The Ndembu are a highly fissile group maintaining order even in van Gennep's "states" only with difficulty. Turner speaks of "the fruitful contest of the sexes," [7] but gives far more attention to conflict in the "social dramas" which mark Ndembu life. [8]

At the end of the day the girl is carried to a seclusion hut at the edge of the village. She will remain here for weeks, even months, being instructed in the knowledge an Ndembu woman is required to have. She will be instructed by senior women, not including her mother. The mother is losing her daughter, giving her to the wider world of marriage and the matrilineage. The girl has been chosen for Nkang'a because her breasts are considered to have developed sufficiently for her to suckle a child. She has left the state of girlhood and begun the process of becoming a woman. On this first day of Nkang'a she is clearly "betwixt and between" states. She has not arrived anywhere.

One detail of the rite compensates the mother. The women run to her hut and place mudyi leaves in the thatch. This is to represent the many grandchildren the mother can expect from losing her daughter.

The girl continues her abnormal life. Whenever possible she adopts a closed position, bending into a foetal stoop and clasping her arms or hands over her ears. Men avoid her. Even to see her would bring certain failure to hunters. This girl is dangerous; she has been set apart. She is now in the marginal phase of the rite of passage.

The aggregation phase sees the female return to normal society. For an Ndembu, this is a great day. Nkang'a finishes with a triumphant demonstration of womanhood. The former girl dances, stomping so that her dress will fall and show her developed breasts. She is given the chief's wand of office for the day. Her husband-to-be is present and the day often concludes with the couple's marriage. The rite of passage is over. She who entered it as a girl, leaves it as a woman.

Turner was fascinated by the marginal phase of the rite, the betwixt and between stage. At Nkang'a this was marked by seclusion and by a mysteriously dangerous quality. The boys' initiation rituals had these marks, too. An additional feature was equality. Girls were initiated singly, boys in groups. Within these groups there was no distinction of rank, no matter what the status of the parents.

Structure and anti-structure

Turner began to speculate that life contained two styles of being in the world. The first he termed "structure." The emphasis here is on order. Structure is concerned with rank, status, position and the expectations which society attaches to these. The most general term used for the second style is "anti-structure." This exists where people step over the threshold (Latin—limen) of structural life into a "liminal" state.

> It is as though there are here two major "models" for human interrelatedness, juxtaposed and alternating. The first is of society as a structured, differentiated, and often hierarchical system of politico-legal-economic positions with many types of evaluation, separating men in terms of "more" or "less." The second, which emerges recognizably in the liminal period, is of society as an unstructured or rudimentarily structured and relatively undifferentiated comitatus, community, or even communion of equal individuals who submit together to the general authority of the ritual elders. [9]

Turner's structure/anti-structure distinction can be extremely helpful to ritualists. It provides a tool for the analysis of a ritual's meaning. One can ask, "What is this ritual about? Is the emphasis on structure, or anti-structure?" Further, the distinction gives a framework for planners. The question now becomes: "What emphasis do we want in this ritual—structure or anti-structure?" But let's look at the two terms of the distinction, structure and anti-structure, more closely.

Structure

First, let me expand the term, "structure." Telephone books are about structure: name, address, number. "Name" is an identity tag, nothing to do with "This is the name by which God has called you." "Address" locates a person. The telephone book gives no indications as to the scenic beauty or lack of it which the address enjoys. Of course, in real estate terms this can become a structure issue; desirable addresses are a sign of economic status or social class, again elements of structure.

Filling out application forms is a classic exercise in structure. The blanks to be filled are like a grid which situates a person in society. Name, address and telephone number identify and locate, as before. "Sex" classifies by gender, "religion" by religious grouping, "age" by years of life. Clearly these classifications are more fuzzy. What of transsexuals? Does "Roman Catholic" indicate baptism in a Catholic church, or weekly Mass attendance, or both? What does "Church of England" indicate? Does "50 years" indicate that one is "past it" or still a valued member of the workforce? But, no matter how imprecise, classifications are important from the perspective of structure, for structure tries to organize things.

This organization appears where we sometimes do not expect it. Romantic love, unconditioned and of the heart, is surely a phenomenon of anti-structure. Yes, but the moment we move to place expectations on the lovers we move towards structure. Thus marriage imposes structure. The lovers now become "husband" and "wife" and, perhaps, "father" and "mother." They move into the complex structure of kinship ties. [10] They have roles within this structure, roles which impose obligations, duties and expectations. Of course, the lovers may be the ones who begin to impose structure. As soon as they begin to think in terms of rights and responsibilities, structure will appear. Undiluted anti-structure, as we shall see, is often a very temporary affair.

The wisdom of age is traditionally thought to bring a view of life which involves more than structure. This may or may not be so. But if the "elder" is seen as a person of authority with clear powers and consequent obligations, the emphasis is on structure again. It may be, of course, that age is being used to classify people as "less" rather than "more" in Western societies. We are beginning to see the evil of putting people down because of their low economic status, race, color, physical disability or even gender.

Perhaps the newest form of intolerance is towards the aged or aging. The tendency to write off those who begin to sprout gray hairs is one more form of intolerance based on structure. Of course they can fight back by getting organized: GRAY POWER political parties, for instance!

But why are the aged written off? Why do they have to fight back? There are many possible reasons but one is that they are too slow. Structure involves organizing time. It deals with deadlines and due dates. It sets times in which tasks are to be done, and the slow are very often at a disadvantage. Punctuality is one of structure's great virtues. Here, the aged may do rather better than they are given credit for, because it seems to me that the older person is very often on time. He or she may do less than younger counterparts, but they do it in an organized fashion. But organized time, whether the time is pressured or more relaxed, is a feature of structure.

Structure may not appear attractive. Order, classification, organization sound like dull routine, the sort of thing most of us are mired in every day, and from which we would love to escape. But structure is necessary. Without it there would be no planned co-operative effort; nothing would ever get done. We like to think we could live a life of total relaxation, but this is wishful thinking. There is a part of us that likes "to get on with it." We feel it after a long vacation. It is the sense of satisfaction we get from harnessing our energies to get some task done. And this is structure.

So there is room for the organizer, the planner, the achiever. The person at the top, who is walled behind a desk, and issues orders from a high status role can be a valuable organizer. He or she is an unattractive figure because of the appearance as some form of "pure structure," unrelieved by traces of other ways of living.

Structure often comes into its own at times of crisis. The structure-oriented person is dependable. Such people go "by the book," and so can be trusted to be honest and reliable. In normal life they may be "dull dogs," but, again, that is a stereotype. Even the "straightest" person may relax into other ways of being than structure.

Anti-structure

The notion of anti-structure takes us beyond simplistic explanations of ritual. As we have seen it can be useful to regard ritual as ". . . a mechanism that periodically converts the obligatory into the desirable." [11] Rituals are rarely as clear-cut as this formula indicates. They can be about more than achieving social order. Rites of passage point to another reality beyond order, the liminal, the marginal, anti-structure. This concept of anti-structure is enormously complex. A key is to see it as the reverse of structure. This negative definition is some help, but there are many ways of moving out of order. Some are destructive; some are ennobling; all are dangerous.

These other ways of being in the world attracted Turner. He found some of them in the marginal phase of rites of passage. He found others being lived by various "way out" groups throughout history: the early Franciscans, assorted millenarian movements, and the Haight-Ashbury hippies. He gave various names to these ways of living. They were all "liminal," requiring a step over the threshold of the "structure" room, a step which led to another space altogether. The most general name for this other way of being in the world was, simply, "anti-structure." [12]

Types of anti-structure

Once a religious educator decides to emphasize anti-structure in ritual, the next question is: what types of anti-structure? There is no need to construct a tight grid of anti-structure types here, but it will be useful to point out some forms of anti-structure that can be helpful in religious education, and some forms that are not.

DANGEROUS TYPES

One property of anti-structure is that it often deals with images of death. It requires a death to the ordinary world, to structure. Thus, the place of initiation for Ndembu girls, the foot of the mudyi tree, is "the place of dying." Anti-structure is also "polluting," a term borrowed from Mary Douglas. [13] So, the secluded girl in Nkang'a must be avoided by hunters. She will bring bad luck. These concepts can be put together to make the point that anti-structure is dangerous, at least from the perspective of structure.

Some forms of anti-structure seem obviously dangerous. They are at one end of the continuum: dangerous—harmless. Moving into drug-induced trances would be one such form. This is common enough in some religious traditions, but it is not a form Christian religious educators are likely to use. Of course, the trance state can be brought on by other methods than drug-taking.

The fascinating BBC documentary film, "The Dervishes of Kurdistan", shows rituals in which devout Kurds move into trance by rhythmic chanting of the holy name, Allah, and by hyperventilation. In these trances they handle venomous snakes, chew glass, take high voltages of electricity through their bodies and pierce their cheeks with skewers—all without coming to apparent harm. Their leader, the sheik, moves among them giving or refusing permission for their "acts of devotion." He is very much the structure figure, the calm assessor of each man's capacities. Even in this extreme form of anti-structure, there is structure. As noted before, undiluted anti-structure is rare.

The taking of alcohol is one more form of moving into trance. Like other forms of drug-taking it is likely to be an enemy of Christian religious educators. It seems less dangerous than other forms of drugs, but its "social aspect" makes it a powerful enemy. Consuming large amounts of alcohol quickly has become a "test of manhood" in various university initiations. As I write, a U.S. university is anguished by the death of a young man in one such ritual.

Another worrying problem is the apparent belief among many men in Western societies that drunkenness is the only acceptable way into anti-structure. Artistic, religious and relational forms are rejected as effeminate. Only alcohol can bring relief from ordered existence; it can bring on oblivion, or lead to noisy camaraderie. This camaraderie may depend on the liminality alcohol brings. The thinly veiled antagonism between men is relaxed as they let their guard down while drinking. Hence "not to drink with me" is an insult because it indicates that you do not trust me enough to lose control, by means of alcohol, in my presence.

Religious educators have work to do in convincing men that there are other ways into anti-structure besides drunkenness. There is a stereotype of the harmless drunk, but excessive consumption of alcohol is too dangerous to be a joke. It not only breaks out of structure but can also destroy it by leading to family violence and other forms of deep disorder.

One challenge that religious educators must face is the provision of less dangerous forms of anti-structure, "less dangerous" because anti-structure is always dangerous from the perspective of structure; it is never harmless. It has a subversive element in it which questions order and routine. This subversive element can be a good thing, but "structureniks" will see it as disturbing in some way or other.

PLAYFUL RITUALS

The subversive element of anti-structure appears in certain rituals where a "ludic" or play aspect is featured. Sometimes there is robust joking or more calculated satire, as in many Mardi Gras or

Carnival celebrations. Sometimes the ludic intent is more serious. Turner's analysis of Chihamba, an Ndembu ritual, shows this serious side. [14] At Chihamba, participants are placed in situations intended to destroy their religious assumptions. They are forced to smash a pot which is hidden under a flour-covered blanket, but they do not know that it is only a pot. They are told it is the skull of Kavula, a grandfather spirit revered among the Ndembu. Later they are made to run about in confusion and then asked a set of impossible questions. Logical answers are laughed out of court by the ritual adapts; idiotic answers are applauded.

Chihamba is merely one example of those rituals which "grind down" social order. These are rituals where ordeals, hassling or ridicule take structure apart and grind it to dust. But the rituals do not end there. After the destructive stage, people can be asked to make new building blocks out of the dust. They are asked to rethink structure, to see what really matters in it. [15]

Official Christianity has never been strong in such rituals. The pre-Lenten revels allowed some criticism of the established religion, though the target of ridicule was usually "structure people," authorities who, because of power or status, were normally beyond public ridicule. But religion was taken more seriously. It was beyond joking. This may well have been because, in many parts of Europe at least, official Christianity's position has not been all that secure. Folk religion in one form or another has been a strong rival. [16] Hence, to allow public ridicule of the official religion may have been thought too dangerous.

Contemporary religious educators do not seem ready to move into subversive attacks on the more pompous aspects of established Christianity. Perhaps now, more than before, the issues are too touchy to be brought into the open.

But there is a need to relax our Christian seriousness. If a religion becomes too fixed in structure, it is dead. Rigor mortis has set in. There needs to be some softening of structure, some playing about with the "deadly serious." This allows flexibility in approaches to time-honored teachings. It allows an openness to change. Perhaps we can grind the whole thing to dust, and build anew. The new building might just preserve what is really important. So there is worth in fun rituals, in role plays, in games that set the imagination free. [17] Religious educators can introduce these things, with difficulty into the official liturgy, with more ease into classroom or home rituals.

Sample Rituals

The following is an attempt to introduce something different into official liturgy. Instead of gospel reading and homily, Tricia Ryan's parish came up with this alternative in the Christmas liturgy.

PRESENTATION OF WORD: Several characters move from congregation to the side of the altar, where they begin to assemble the classic Nativity Scene. Whilst they are assembling the scene they start to grumble:

"Same as always!"; "Every Christmas we have to do this"; "Why do we bother with all this rubbish!" etc. etc.

PRIEST: "Well, hold on, what does Christmas mean to you then?"

Characters freeze in their positions of construction, then one by one each steps away from the group and turns to audience to say what Christmas means to them. As each character finishes and comes back to group there is a brief continuation of construction, then freeze again while the next character goes out to audience.

BUSINESS MAN: "Christmas? Christmas is big business, it's a time for making lots of money, ha, ha, ha. Sapping people in with slogans about peace and love and goodwill on earth, ha! What a gimmick—Christmas is great!"

LONELY PERSON: (Heavy sigh) "Christmas used to be such a fun time—we'd have a beautiful plum pudding and . . . oh, so many things. (Pause) Nobody comes for Christmas anymore!" (Looks quizzically at audience then goes back to group)

PARTY-GOER: (With slurs!) "Christmas is 'triffic! Party after party after party after... Then there's New Year!!!"

CHILD: (Excited) "Last year I got a BMX bike from Grandma, an' a new truck from Uncle Bill, an' this year I want...an' I want...an' I wan' ...an' I, an' I..."

SANTA CLAUS: "Ho, ho, bloody ho! Kids! Christmas! Spending all day in a fur coat with grotty kids putting lollies in my beard and demanding to be kissed and cuddled and wanting this and that and..."

HARASSED MUM: "Christmas, I'll never know why they ever invented it! Cooking twenty hours a day, oh, and I still haven't got a present for Tony, oh, and there's Aunty Joan and oh goodness, Grandma said she wouldn't come for another two days—how am I going to get the time to do everything!"

After she has returned to the group and they continue building nativity scene, suddenly from the back:

JESUS: "Is that what it's all about, is it?" Characters look at each other as Jesus walks to the front; he gestures towards the characters but speaks to the congregation:
                     "Is this what you've made of my birth?"

N.B. Nativity scene should be finished by the time Jesus first speaks.

TO FINISH: Jesus walks off in disgust, followed by other characters who obviously want to know more!

The modern Christmas dilemma which Tricia has designed leads obviously into discussion either in the liturgy or after it. The structure of religion is relaxed in the sense that people other than the officiating clergy are invited to have a say.

Let's now take an example of a nonliturgical ritual. The following is really a complex of rituals designed by a group of women, including Bev Zimmerman. Here is Bev's account of what happened:

> The celebration began with a period of quiet followed by a naming of ourselves and the identification of those women in our lives with whom we have had a mother-daughter relationship. These women could be associated biologically as in mother, grandmother, or aunt or in a figurative way, that is spiritually, historically, biblically etc. or any combination of these. Each of us spoke of some of the qualities and characteristics of the women we named. For example, I am . . . daughter of Joan who has shown me what it is to trust; daughter of Ruth who has shown me what it is to be a religious woman etc. The exercise was a unique way of telling our own story, of acknowledging the gifts that others had shared with us and of sharing insights about ourselves.

> We then dispensed with words and entered more deeply into a process which became for each of us a healing process. Using only gestures and body movement we expressed to a partner (chosen at random) some past barrier which had prevented us from becoming fully human. The partner expressed, again in gesture and movement, a response to what she had seen. The partners could then talk about the experience. For me this was a special component of the celebration. Even though I felt exposed and vulnerable, I also felt support and acceptance.

> The high point of the celebration occurred when some members of the group decided that they would make and bake the bread which would form the basis of the meal. This whole process was ritualised in the following way. The bread-making group returned to the total group with the

baked bread and placed it on the table. They came also with flour-covered hands and the utensils used and proceeded to wash up in silence in front of the group. This gesture was meant to acknowledge the service done by women, so often in silence and behind the scenes. One member of the group then shared the recipe with the others beginning—A reading from Mother's Choice Flour . . . This was accompanied by some interchange as some women asked for the finer points of the recipe.

The group entered more deeply into the ritual. Each woman was asked to break the bread. This was done either in silence or with some formula expressing the brokenness of the individual or of some other woman. After some time this fairly intense period was broken by someone asking, spontaneously, if anyone would like a cup of tea or coffee. Finally, the group sat around in a very relaxed fashion and had afternoon tea.

This is a serious enough set of rituals, but note how quietly subversive it is. It does not accept that men officiate at ritual. It celebrates the "subjugated language" of women in our society where, unlike the Ndembu, we have stressed patrilineage, not matrilineage. There are moments too, where high seriousness goes out the window, such as the exchange of the bread recipe.

Bev's ritual has structure, of course; it is planned. But how people will react cannot be planned. So, I feel, this ritual is mainly about anti-structure; it invites a move into the liminal. The liminal here is "intense" to use Bev's word. Expressing one's brokenness is a threat to our normal structure mask which gives the message that we have everything under control. To admit that we have been out of control is not easy, and we cannot stay in such a frightening place of the heart for too long. So the "cuppa" brings relief. It breaks the intensity and the women are able to "come to the surface" again with relaxed talk.

LIMINOID ANTI-STRUCTURE

It can be argued that these "liminal rituals" are rare in our societies, that the subversive element in ritual has largely moved to art, music and theater. People in these fields criticize accepted values. The process often begins on the margins of society; criticism comes from the fringe personalities. It is sometimes rejected and the art or music or drama "fails." Sometimes it hits a nerve and audiences recognize that the criticism is just, that this piece of structure or that deserves to be ground to dust and rebuilt in a different shape. Then, what began on the margins, moves to the center. It may become a classic. People then move into anti-structure by being "rapt" in its beauty. Perhaps they do not even recognize that once this work of art shocked the establishment so much that it could have been rejected as too dangerous.

The term "liminoid" is used for this artistic form of anti-structure. It is more fragmentary and quirky than tribal rituals. It depends on the insights of artists, and these may or may not be deeply perceptive. The great tribal rituals plunge people into liminality knowing that there are important values that will triumph. Such ritual complexes are still around in modern societies. Easter, with its insistence that life will conquer death, is one such. But we depend more and more on the artist. The perspective of the artist may be individual so that we need be critical of its subversiveness; but we must attend to the artists in our society if we are to pick up criticisms of structure that need to be made. [18]

This is another task for religious educators. They must be concerned that art, music, drama, and literature be part of the education process. Religious education needs to be strongly focused on anti-structure, but at this point it is worth stressing the involvement it should have with one form of anti-structure, the subversively artistic. The artist can point to what is genuinely human by exposing the superficialities of structure. It is necessary that people have roles in society, but they are more than their roles. The artist awakens our sensitivity to this "other dimension." Without such sensitivity there can be no genuine concern for other human beings. Neither can there be any possibility of openness to God. [19]

RELATIONAL ANTI-STRUCTURE (COMMUNITAS)

The relational form of anti-structure receives quite a deal of attention in anthropological writings. It occurs when people step out of their roles and communicate on a "person-to-person" basis. When a father and his adult son can communicate as equals, anti-structure is achieved. So, too, when "superiors" and "subordinates" forget rank and talk openly about personal matters, they move into anti-structure. The term, communitas, is used to describe this "community, or even communion of equal individuals." [20]

Communitas can be any human relationship where people step out of their roles and relate as persons. It can describe something as simple as a shared joke between strangers, the flash of recognition when two train travelers see something funny and catch each other's eye. It can be the heart-to-heart talk between spouses or friends, usually in the kitchen. It "emerges where social structure is not," [21] in the sense that communitas is not about structure but about personal values. It can go very deep:

> The kind of communitas desired by tribesmen in their rites and by hippies in their "happenings" is not the pleasurable and effortless comradeship that can arise between friends, coworkers, or professional colleagues any day. What they seek is a transformative experience that goes to the root of each person's being and finds in that root something profoundly communal and shared. [22]

In general, anthropologists are interested in these "trans-formative experiences" more than in the small change of daily interactions. This may be unfortunate, but it is understandable. The extreme forms of communitas have provided fascinating studies for cultural anthropology.

One such study deals with Francis of Assisi, seen as a quintessential liminar, breaking away from family ties, wealth, and status by stripping off the clothes his father had given him, and entering a life of poverty and communitas. [23] This communitas consisted of close unstructured relationships with his friars and a burning, passionate love of Christ. Francis had no patience with structure and no skills in its ways. He abhorred property and the structures of business which came with it. He was incapable of writing a rule which gave clear canonical definition of his friars' role in the Church. The superficialities of large group relationships were not for him, and, so, he spent his final years moving from one small community of friars to another.

As the friars multiplied and Francis's movement became more and more "successful," the need for structure grew. Rome wanted to know precisely what the new group was about. Thought had to be given to the education of the friars, to caring for the sick and aging friars—to structure. Francis's successor, Elias, was a "structure person." He organized the order. Significantly, it was he who built the basilica at Assisi which houses Francis's body. "With Elias, structure, both material and abstract, had begun to replace communitas." [24]

Lambert's summation of Elias's work is even harsher: ". . . he made a more lasting contribution to the development of the city (of Assisi) than ever he did to the evolution of the Franciscan ideal." [25] Here structure comes out badly, but it is worth emphasizing again the balance needed. Anti-structure, particularly communitas, will appeal to many religious educators, but it needs structure. Communitas is attractive: it "is richly charged with affects," it "has something magical about it . . . the feeling of endless power." [26] But this power untransformed cannot readily be applied to the organizational details of social existence. It is no substitute for lucid thought and sustained will. Wisdom is always to find the appropriate relationship between structure and communitas under the given circumstances of time and place, to accept each modality when it is paramount without rejecting the other, and not to cling to one when its present impetus is spent.

The religious educator will need wisdom to recognize the time when structure should be emphasized and the time when a change to a modality of communitas is due. But communitas deserves the greater emphasis over all. It deserves this because it is a peculiarly Christian form of anti-structure. It does not emphasize the ecstatic, the riotous or the angry. All these can be Christian forms of anti-structure, but they very often are not. Communitas stresses the acceptance of persons as persons. It asks that I and another person communicate honestly about matters that are important to us at a deep level. This is a form of anti-structure that is totally consonant with Jesus' teachings. It does not gloss over conflict by shifting attention to structured ritual, but insists that the more important need is heartfelt reconciliation. (Mt. 5:23 ff.) It directs attention to people: to women, to wives, to business partners, and to enemies. These people are to be treated as persons and not to be put into some category where structure codifies their "rights." (Mt.5:27 ff.)

Communitas is central to Christianity, and Matthew's "sermon on the mount" expresses this centrality. Jesus was challenged because he practised communitas. "Why does he eat with tax collectors and sinners?" (Mk. 2:16) How could this teacher ignore the structures of the Jewish society of his time, and live in communitas with social outcasts, eating with them and including them among his "followers"? (Mk. 2:15) The question is important as it highlights Jesus' insistence on a modality of communitas. The approach of a Christian religious educator would seem to need the same insistence.

Warning noises have to be made again, of course. It is a Christian ideal that persons be treated as persons. This does not mean that they are required to bare their souls on demand. Well-meaning insistence on a communitas model can invade privacy; the person is forced to take a truth drug rather than being treated as a person.

The work of religious education is to encourage communitas rather than to demand it. People need situations in which they feel safe to be themselves. Religious educators can provide these situations by adopting forms of leadership that treat persons as persons rather than as students, inferiors or some other unit of structure. This at least sets up the opportunity for those being educated to relate at depth with the educator; or, perhaps more importantly, for those being educated to relate at depth with one another. The aim of the religious educator is not, after all, to become the indispensable focus for communitas. Thinking one is indispensable is structure gone mad. The true aim of the religious educator is the growth of those being educated. It is important that these persons become aware of who they are and of their relation to God.

As one religious educator, John Shea, puts it, I find my religious identity, who I am in the last analysis, by telling my story over and over again. [27] But telling my story requires communitas. I need people who will listen, with love and with creative challenging. And they need me to listen to their stories. Bev Zimmerman's ritual shows how people can be helped to tell their stories in an atmosphere that affirms them. This is true communitas.

This form of communitas sounds much more ordinary than some of the anthropological examples. There may be only the simplest of rituals assisting and achieving communication, and none of the drama, drugs and music of tribal or hippie examples. But the important thing about communitas is not that it seems "new" to people, or that it is rich in effect. The important thing is that it helps people be themselves so that they can grow in an atmosphere where they feel they belong.

Communitas can very quickly change to structure. There is nothing sinister in this. We are all familiar with the joke or change of subject that signals that we, or someone in our group, have had enough of communicating at depth and that it is time to leave a communitas mode for chit-chat or business as usual. The "cuppa" at the end of Bev's ritual illustrates this in action. There are also generational changes—Francis's communitas changes to Elias's structure.

It is almost a rule of human nature that movements which begin by breaking away from structure move back into it quickly, certainly within one generation. The Franciscan movement is an example, as are more modern groups; the hippies and the flower people of the sixties. And we can jump to the punks of the seventies and eighties. These groups begin as revolts against structure. They quickly—some of them very quickly—evolve their own structures: dress, behavior, hierarchy that must be accepted. The new structure is often more dictatorial than the old. So what appears to be spontaneous communitas can use its appearance to oppress people with awesome efficiency. I suspect that some charismatic groups have achieved exactly this kind of efficiency.

There are many other forms of anti-structure. We can move away from roles, expectations and status on a relaxed vacation or by going for long walks alone. We can become absorbed in some activity that either allows us to drift into waking dreams or which focuses our attention so strongly that we forget all the demands of structure. We can leave structure in quiet meditation. We can feel "lost" and very much out of structure in the busiest airport terminal where, all our usual supports gone, we feel that we belong to no one. Some forms of anti-structure—the "flow" of a speed-skater or distance runner, the passion of the Berlin Philharmonic playing Beethoven—seem set about with rules and demands which somehow free people and lift them out of structure. [28] Anti-structure is part of the process of life. We move to and fro between structure and anti-structure, unsure where to settle.

This element of opposition needs stressing. As Charles Leslie remarks, the opposition between structure and anti-structure is as important as that between life and death instincts in Freud. [29] But, besides this "either/or" element there is also a "both/and" element. Structure and anti-structure exist side by side, they co-exist, they even co-depend.

So the great ice hockey player or racing jockey cannot be lost in action without the framework of the contest which structure provides. The conductor of a symphony orchestra provides order and also stirs passionate rendition. The ecstatic behavior of the dervishes of Kurdistan cannot begin unless the sheik, the descendant of the Prophet, gives the permission which "legitimates" the behavior.

RELIGIOUS ANTI-STRUCTURE

The relationship of structure and anti-structure is, then, a complicated one. One more form of anti-structure which needs consideration is religious anti-structure. The ritual of the Kurds is clearly an example of religious anti-structure. There is a move into anti-structure which has direct religious motivation as its base and which produces behavior expressly recognized as devotion to Allah. The methods of moving into ecstatic anti-structure, hyperventilation and rhythmic chant, are, however, physiologically based.

All this points to both the glory and the pain of religious anti-structure. It can express deep faith and extraordinary love of God and it can also lead to excesses of frenzy or to blatant quackery. Yet it is possible, I believe, to find forms of religious anti-structure acceptable to the sanest of religious educators.

Sample Ritual

Michael Horsley has given me a ritual outline which is clearly sane. I find religious educators have no difficulty seeing themselves use such a ritual. It is designed as a pre-Confirmation ritual, assuming that the sacrament is celebrated towards the end of primary schooling. It could just as easily be used as a rite of passage between child and young adult stages:

> The ritual begins with the parents and initiates, hand in hand, walking in and out of the church several times symbolising the example and encouragement given in the faith since Baptism. The time has now come for the initiates to take up the responsibility of their own faith. At the back of the church they break from the parents and proceed alone to the sanctuary. The rite of separation culminates in the putting on of a white alb or gown tied at the waist (reflections of Baptism where the parents/godparents clothed the initiate in a similar garment representing the putting on of Christ. Now the initiates place the gown on themselves—symbolic of assuming the responsibility for their own faith).

> The liminal period has begun, the marginal state. The initiates proceed to the altar and touch the chalice of wine and the bread, symbolic of the root metaphor containing the paschal mystery—Eucharist. They then proceed to the priest who signs them with the cross of forgiveness and the blessing of the Holy Spirit. These symbolic actions reflect the responsibility they now have to nourish their own faith with the Eucharist and Reconciliation. The initiates then leave the church.

> The precincts of the church grounds represent the world. Throughout the grounds there are people in different situations in life: a boy in scant clothing sitting alone, a girl in a wheelchair, a lady carrying a heavy load, sick people, a mum washing up, a dad in the garden, a puppy needing care, plants needing water and people needing to be embraced. Those being cared for are from many different ethnic backgrounds indicating the multicultural aspect of our society. As the initiates wander through their symbolic world they are required to help anyone they encounter, receiving a small token from each person. This token represents the person helped and the responsibility one has to help and care for all people and take them to the Lord.

After each initiate has encountered several people they then
return to the church, passing the priest who places his hands
on their head, and proceeding to the altar place their tokens
upon it (their encounters). These two actions speak of the
continual need to return to the sacraments for spiritual
nourishment—Reconciliation and Eucharist: and further
highlights the root metaphor which encompasses all
encounters. The parents are in the body of the church to
welcome the initiates to the community. The white gown is
removed and the initiates join their parents and leave the
church, aggregated to a new role, that of an adult Christian.

The point I wish to make is that this ritual invites a move to
"contact with God." There are actions, gestures, short times for
reflection which could lead these initiates to experience a sense of
God's presence. I am not saying that this will happen, only that it
can. The ritual opens towards the sacred, it invites a move to
religious anti-structure. It invites, but probably no one, except
those participating in the ritual, will ever know if the invitation
was accepted or not.

The basis for religious forms of anti-structure is the "other"
dimension hinted at in Michael's ritual, and called on more
dramatically in the Chihamba ritual. This latter ritual clearly goes
beyond notions of social control. It deliberately undermines the
accepted beliefs of Ndembu society and religion in its attempt to
insist that there is something beyond human ken at the base of
religion. This "mystery" is fundamental to religious anti-structure.
Once a human being contacts this mystery in a profound way, the
person would seem to be out of structure, to be apart from the
usual demands of structured living.

Anti-structure in the Christian tradition

Mystery is at the heart of Christianity. Theologians have always
insisted that the God of Christianity cannot be fitted into human
categories. Bernard Lonergan continues the tradition. He explains
that our love of God is, logically, topsy-turvey. We love first,

without understanding who it is we love. As our love grows, we understand more, but the greatest saint is nowhere near "knowing God." [30]

Karl Rahner makes the same point when he stresses the absolutely fundamental importance of mystery and transcendence:

> mystery in its incomprehensibility is what is self-evident in human life. If transcendence is not something which we practice on the side as a metaphysical luxury of our intellectual existence, but if this transcendence is rather the plainest, most obvious and most necessary condition of possibility for all spiritual understanding and comprehension, then the holy mystery really is the one thing that is self-evident, the one thing which is grounded in itself even from our point of view. For all other understanding, however clear it might appear, is grounded in this transcendence. All clear understanding is grounded in the darkness of God. [31]

The theologians are simply developing notions central to the resource documents of Christianity, the scriptures. The God of the Exodus cannot be "seen" by human beings: "You cannot see my face, for man cannot see me and live." (Ex. 33:19) Job's challenge to God ends with: "I have been holding forth on matters I cannot understand." (Jb. 42:3)

The Jesus of the New Testament has this quality of mystery far more than popular devotional material allows. The eerie episode of the Gerasene demoniac frightens people so much that they want Jesus to leave their neighborhood. (Mk.5:17) Jesus' parables often defy logic by pointing to a God who refuses to accept a structure view of life as normative. So the owner of the vineyard pays late-comers a full wage. His generosity is quite illogical and leads, in Matthew, to the paradox: ". . . the last will be first, and the first, last." (Mt. 20:16) Clear understanding of scripture is, then, firmly grounded in "the darkness of God."

It is tempting to accept a romantic vision of Jesus as an anti-structure figure. Serious scholars come close to this. Ferdinand Hahn presents a Jesus who is impatient with the ossified version of Judaism presented by the Pharisees and by the temple priesthood.

Hahn emphasizes Jesus' rejection of the sabbath rest: "The sabbath was made for man, not man for the sabbath," (Mk.2:27), and his repudiation of ritual cleanliness: "Nothing that goes into a man from outside can make him unclean; it is the things that come out of a man that make him unclean." (Mk.7:15) The expulsion of buyers, sellers and animals from the temple is, for Hahn, "a symbolic act" indicating Jesus' rejection of cultic worship. Jesus repudiates Jewish observance of the law and its concomitant ritualization of life, and he proclaims the end of the temple cult. [32]

The meals of Jesus are, for Hahn, another sign of his break with structure. Jesus refuses to divide the world into sacred and profane sectors. Every person and thing is open to God's saving action. Worship, then, is not to be confined to cultic actions in cult places:

> Jesus' repasts thus reveal quite concretely the significance of his conduct with respect to the liturgical ordinances of Judaism: here all ritual precepts are set aside by virtue of sovereign authority, all walls separating the sacred from the profane are torn down. These acts of table fellowship take place in the midst of daily life, and no one remains excluded from the act of worship. [33]

Hahn sees this trend as continuing in the early Christian communities. Words which later denote worship, such as leitourgia (liturgy), do not have this function in the early New Testament texts. [34] The terminology indicates that the communities did not distinguish between acts of worship and acts of service. The walls between sacred and profane had not been rebuilt.

Yet it is very clear that the walls were rebuilt, and quickly. Things were organized. A scholar such as Josef Jungmann seems to delight in this organization:

> What had been at the Last Supper a proclamation and anticipation of Jesus' sacrificial death was now to be memorialized. . . serious decisions had to be taken. In what framework and setting should the memorial be celebrated? on what occasions? in what group of participants? Should it be presided over by an official with a special mandate, or celebrated simply at a round table of equals? [35]

These questions were answered with a bias towards structure. The liturgy became formalized, restrictions were enforced to exclude sinners and a new cult came into being. There is no use bewailing the developments. They may very well have been totally justified by the circumstances. Jesus may have favored anti-structure because that was appropriate in his circumstances. The later New Testament writers, followed by Justin and Hippolytus, may have recorded a necessary change in emphasis. There is a need for balance in applying the distinction between structure and anti-structure.

For all that, there is a sense in which Hahn must have the better of the argument. Jesus is a teacher and leader, clearly structure roles. But he does stress anti-structure. His disciples are to remember that leadership requires that they wash feet, that they serve. (Jo.13: 12–16) Even more fundamentally, Jesus announces the coming of the Kingdom of God. He proclaims the good news that God is actively present among us. This means that human structures are being challenged by God's presence. No matter how important these structures are, God's action is infinitely more important. God may use structures but God will not be bound by them. They are, from a Christian perspective, of secondary importance. Structure, in the presence of Mystery and Love, must be secondary. Religious anti-structure must be central to Christianity.

It is possible to ignore religious anti-structure. One can build an enormous edifice of rational theology with God as base: there is a God, who sent Jesus, who founded a Church, which teaches... and one can tinker with the theological structure forever while ignoring the base. The mystery of God, blazing out at Sinai and at Easter, can be tamed and domesticated. But all this seems a betrayal of Christianity, and of religion. It would seem that religious educators need to take religious anti-structure seriously. Somewhere they have to look at the possibility that they, or those they educate, or both might have some experience of God. They have to consider prayer and meditation as having some relevance for the enterprise of religious education.

I broach the subject carefully. I am not pushing any particular religious barrow, but it seems to me that the notion of anti-structure pushes religious educators into this corner. I suspect that many religious educators share Thomas Geoghegan's fear of those who admit to praying: "I admired my courage, getting involved with people who might turn out to be religious fanatics, preaching in tongues or handling snakes." [36] But if religion admits, in fact insists, that there is a God or transcendent being of some kind who is beyond human structuring, one form of anti-structure would seem to involve any honest dealings we have with that God.

What to do about these dealings in religious education will be left for the next chapter where two possible forms of "religious experience" will be discussed. One, a clear move into liminal space to contact God, may be for some. The other, a recognition that God acts in the most ordinary of events, should be for all. At this point some conclusions about the relation between structure and anti-structure can be made.

A question of balance

Perhaps the most obvious conclusion is that it is incorrect to categorize structure as "bad" and anti-structure as "good." Balanced Christian living needs both. Structure can be so rigid that it prevents any form of human growth. Yet, without structure, anti-structure can be so dangerous that it destroys. Anti-structure and true religion would seem very similar phenomena. Both are concerned with love of God and neighbor. But love can easily degenerate into sentiment or escalate into frenzy. Structure prevents this. Its place is, then, as a tool or servant for anti-structure. It is necessary, but subordinate in religious matters. That is, religion is concerned fundamentally with anti-structure but needs structure to achieve balance. If structure becomes an end in itself, religion loses its true purpose.

Structure and anti-structure should co-exist. It is probably inevitable that we human beings will stress one, then the other. We will become bored with order and lurch into disorder. When this frightens us or paralyzes us for productive activity, we will scramble back to structure. Ideally, the two should go together, each controlling the excesses of the other.

Occasionally we meet a person who seems totally structured. He or she seems to miss out on so much in life, perhaps missing the point of life altogether. We meet the occasional person who seems to live in permanent anti-structure: the drop-out, the beach bum, the hermit. The court jester seemed to have such a role, though the word "role" sounds a warning. Figures of permanent anti-structure may have to become very organized to cope with the loneliness of their position. The clown will weep in private if he or she has not done this work of organization.

Some groups attempt permanent anti-structure, for example, the followers of Francis, the hippies and the flower people. There are more frightening groups one could cite: the anarchists of the early 1900s and today's terrorist organizations. These groups may begin as phenomena of anti-structure, but they rarely remain unstructured for long. Permanent anti-structure is a fantasy. Lotus-eaters have to work, or die. Gypsy horsemen have to elect leaders. Christian communes have to organize or perish. Ease, romance and disorder are not the stuff of permanence.

If anti-structure is never permanent, it is also rarely undiluted. Indeed it is difficult to think of an example of pure anti-structure. Perhaps a totally uninhibited, drunken orgy would be one. I suppose it is possible that one could be held. But I would lay a large bet that it would not be allowed to continue for long. Structure could not tolerate it. The neighbors would complain. Undiluted anti-structure is seldom seen in the land. The conclusion is, then, that structure and anti-structure, for most people, go together. Life is a game of balancing them to get the best result.

This is precisely what religious educators must do. They can analyze rituals that they, or others, have used, and ask: What was the main emphasis, structure or anti-structure? They can go on to question whether the particular emphasis was appropriate or not. In planning ritual, they should ask: What emphasis do we want here; structure or anti-structure? If we want anti-structure, what form of it do we want, and how will we use structure elements to avoid extremes? These questions of analysis and planning need to be asked again and again. In the next chapter I shall examine the mechanics of asking them and answering them. These questions, I believe, best address the issue of meaning in ritual. By asking them we ask: what does this ritual mean? Or, more fully, how have symbols been used to express meaning in this ritual?

Discussion Questions

1.   Think of a rite of passage in your culture.
     Identify in it, if you can, the stages of
     —separation
     —marginalization and
     —reaggregation
     What liminal elements can you detect?

2.   From your experience of each of the following would you
     classify it as emphasising structure or anti-structure?
     —a family meal at Christmas?
     —meditation?
     —jogging?
     —a vacation?
     —a graduation from high school or university?

3.   Reflect on a religious ceremony you have attended. Was the
     emphasis on structure or anti-structure? Would you have
     liked more anti-structure or less? Why?

Notes
   1.   Webb-Mitchell, B., "Rituals in a l'Arche Community," *British Journal
        of Religious Education*, 12/2 (Spring, 1990), 86-93.
   2.   Turner, V., *The Ritual Process*, Ithaca, N.Y.: Cornell University Press,
        1969, p.131. The book contains the Lewis Henry Morgan Lectures
        for 1966.
   3.   Turner, V., "The Anthropology of Performance" in Turner, E. (ed.),
        On the Edge of the Bush, Tucson, Arizona: University of Arizona
        Press, 1985, 177-204. Note particularly Turner's interest in Sally
        Moore's thesis (argued in *Law as Process*, London: Routledge and
        Kegan Paul, 1978), pp.183-4.
   4.   Gennep, Arnold van, *The Rites of Passage*, trans. M. Vizedom and
        G. Caffee, London: Routledge and Kegan Paul, 1909. For Turner's
        use of van Gennep, see *The Ritual Process*, pp.94-5.
   5.   Turner, V., *The Forest of Symbols*, Ithaca, N.Y: Cornell University
        Press, 1967, pp. 23 ff. For more detail, see Turner's *Lunda Rites and
        Ceremonies*, Rhodes-Livingstone Museum Paper, No.10, Livingstone,
        Northern Rhodesia, 1953.
   6.   Rogers, Susan Carol, "Woman's Place: A Critical Review of
        Anthropological Theory," *Comparative Studies in Society and History*,
        20 (1978), 123-63. Harris, H.V.C., "Sexual Attraction: A Test Case of
        Sociobiological Theory," *Zygon*, 19/3 (Sept. 1984), 317-30.

7. Turner, V., *The Ritual Process*, p. 79. In the further discussion (pp. 81 ff.) see the material on cross-sexual joking, particularly as found in the twin ceremony.

8. The "social drama" concept fascinated Turner. He applies it at length to Ndembu society in *Schism and Continuity in an African Society*, Manchester: Manchester University Press, for the Rhodes-Livingstone Institute, 1957.

9. Turner, V., *The Ritual Process*, p.96.

10. A good example of the refusal to structure romantic love is the Sahajiya cult of Bengal. Turner mentions it in *The Ritual Process*, pp.154 ff. Edward Dimock, (*The Place of the Hidden Moon*, Chicago: University of Chicago Press, 1966) gives an excellent treatment.

11. Turner, V., *The Forest of Symbols*, Ithaca, N.Y.: Cornell University Press, 1967.

12. Turner does not use the term a great deal. It appears in the subtitle of *The Ritual Process*: Structure and Anti-structure.

13. Douglas, Mary, *Purity and Danger*, London: Routledge and Kegan Paul, 1966.

14. Turner, V., *Revelation and Divination in Ndembu Ritual*, Ithaca, N.Y.: Cornell University Press, 1975.

15. Turner, V., "Variations on a Theme of Liminality" in Sally F. Moore and Barbara G. Meyerhoff (eds.), *Secular Ritual*, Assen/Amsterdam: Van Gorcum, 1977, p.38.

16. For examples, see Pitt-Rivers, J., *The People of the Sierra*, Chicago: Phoenix, 1969, and *The Fate of Shechem or the Politics of Sex*, Cambridge: C.U.P., 1977.

17. This has, of course, been recognized by many religious educators. The importance of the imagination in religious education is stressed by Maria Harris (*Teaching and Religious Education*, San Francisco: Harper & Row, 1987).

18. Turner, V., "Variations on a Theme of Liminality," 43-5.

19. See Durka, Gloria and Smith, Joanmarie (eds.), *Aesthetic Dimensions of Religious Education*, New York: Paulist Press, 1979.

20. Turner, V., *The Ritual Process*, p.96.

21. *Ibid*. p.126.

22. *Ibid*. p.138.

23. *Ibid*. pp.140 ff.

24. *Ibid*. p.149.

25. *Ibid*. The quotation is from Lambert, M.D., *Franciscan Poverty*, London: Allenson, 1961, p.74.

26. Turner, V., *The Ritual Process*, p.139.

27. Shea, J., "Storytelling and Religious Identity," *Chicago Studies*, 21/1 (Spring 1982), 23-43.

28. For Turner on "flow", see his "Variations on a Theme of Liminality," pp. 46 ff.

29. See Leslie's review of Turner's *The Ritual Process* in *Science*, 168 (1970), 703. Mary Collins gives an excellent discussion of Turner's

"processual view of society" in her "Ritual Symbols and the Ritual Process: The Work of Victor W. Turner," *Worship* 50 (1976), 336-46, particularly p.341.

30. Lonergan, Bernard, *Method in Theology*, New York: Herder & Herder, 1973, pp.115 ff.
31. Rahner, Karl, "Unthematic Knowledge of God," in Gorman, Margaret   (ed.), *Psychology and Religion*, N.Y. : Paulist Press, 1985, pp.7-11.
32. Hahn, Ferdinand, *The Worship of the Early Church*, translated D.E. Green, Philadelphia: Fortress, 1973, pp. 30-1.
33. *Ibid.* p.19.
34. *Ibid.* pp. 36-8.
35. Jungmann, Josef, *The Mass*, translated by Julian Fernandes, Collegeville, Minnesota: The Liturgical Press, 1975, p.17.
36. Geoghegan, Th., "Confessions of a Practicing Catholic," *America*, 158/13 (April 2, 1988), 350-56, 365-6. In particular, p.365.

CHAPTER FIVE

▸ *Structure and Anti-structure —Applications*

A *question of emphasis*

This final chapter applies Turner's theories on meaning in ritual to religious education. There will be little explication of anthropological theory and much more attention to the practical use of ritual in religious education. How can religious educators analyze rituals that have or have not "worked"? How can the structure/anti-structure categories be used to determine what a particular ritual used in religious education can or ought to be about?

The chapter will deal with planning but will digress into presenting rituals which I and other religious educators have used. The rituals are relevant to the points made about planning, but they have their own far greater value. They give more examples of what educators are doing, and any treatment of ritual needs example after example of what can be done!

First, note the point that ritual, even in religious education, can properly stress either structure or anti-structure. Religion has principally to do with anti-structure, but there are occasions when structure will be celebrated, and rightly so. When a principal comes to take charge of a school a number of rituals are used to fix the person into the new role. There are introductions to staff and to parents, gatherings for coffee and cake. These might look like cosy communitas affairs but they really are about showing folk that "this is the new principal"; they are about structure.

The eucharist, too, can have strong elements of structure. Joseph Gelineau pointed, over a decade ago, to statistics indicating that two-thirds of French Catholics did not believe in Christ's resurrection. He argued that such Catholics needed teaching and that certain Masses, not all, should be clearly advertised as providing this teaching at the Liturgy of the Word. [1] Gelineau was proposing that there could be a strong and beneficial structure element in Sunday worship. The homilist would take on the role of teacher, the congregation the role of those being taught.

I have worked on school "camps" where potential class leaders were inducted into their leadership roles for the coming academic year. There was a clear emphasis on structure, though the type of leadership proposed at least edged towards a service model. But educators, particularly religious educators, often use "camp" experiences as occasions for emphasizing anti-structure. How do such occasions work?

First, there is a clear break with the usual structures of life. School is left behind, usually the city is exchanged for the great outdoors. Everyone, including teaching staff, is expected to help with chores. Yesterday's strict disciplinarian seems almost human today. But then what? What is to be achieved by this loosening of the structures? Often, I suspect religious educators are not at all clear about what is to be achieved. Things muddle along, sometimes happily, sometimes not, and everyone goes home tired if not happy.

Suppose some planning is done. If Turner's categories are applied, most religious educators would probably select anti-structure as the primary goal of the experience. What kind of anti-structure? Presumably most would go for either relational or religious anti-structure, or a mixture of both. A mixture may entail difficulties, but compromise is usually the name of the game in planning. So let's see how the planning operation would go.

Suppose the emphasis is on relational anti-structure, or communitas to use the technical word. Here the aim is to foster interaction among students at a human level. We want them interacting as persons, and not from behind the masks of their usual roles as drop-out, clown, do-gooder or victim. Another decision involves staff. Should they act as facilitators of communitas while still remaining structure figures? Or should they move out of their "one-up" position to be part of the communitas process, perhaps bringing in skilled outsiders to act as facilitators?

Once these questions are decided, the strategies to promote communitas must be mapped out at least in some preliminary way. Is it enough to bring people together in a relaxed atmosphere? Is there need for games or role plays which get folk talking about what is really important to them? Perhaps it will be appropriate to put participants through tests of physical endurance or into situations of controlled danger. Experiences of hardship or danger often strip masks away and allow the real person to emerge. This can help the process of revealing our real selves to others. Perhaps the emphasis is on memories of years spent together and strategies will include journal writing or designing of class banners or choosing of group or personal symbols. The facilitator has to be ready with the appropriate strategy.

Flexibility is needed

The facilitating person or team is clearly a structure element. The control and wisdom necessary to balance the emotions set loose in communitas come from this direction. The planning which promotes communitas comes from the facilitators, too, or is implemented by them, but this planning must be flexible. If the aim of the exercise is to move step by step through a plan, we are back in structure; in fact structure has become an end in itself. Planning must help communitas emerge, not replace it.

Sample Ritual

Let me give an example of flexibility in planning. Narelle Mullins has set down her experience of planning an Easter ritual with her five-year-old daughter, Sara. You might think that rituals for five-year-old children have to be thought up by the parent and imposed on the children. But watch this process in action:

The process of how this ritual eventuated is quite clear when documenting it in hindsight. The actual thought processes connected with the Easter Message undoubtedly began in Sara's kindergarten class. Class teaching/talk centered on Jesus and the fact that he died and "came alive again." (Sara!) As well on Holy Thursday the whole school was involved in a liturgy that walked through the last events of Jesus' life.

Kindergarten class activities revolved around the painting of Easter eggs, drawings and Maths activities about chickens and eggs etc. Another significant "step" in the process was an unforeseen one—Sara on Palm Sunday night was chasing her dad when she slipped and fell and cut her head. A quick trip to hospital (with her screaming all the way "I don't want to die!") resulted in six stitches and two days in hospital. During her convalescence, the son of a teacher friend of mine sent her one of his favourite toys to help her get better. It was a well-worn bunny and Sara, who knows well the story of the Velveteen Rabbit by Margery Williams, immediately gave the bunny the name "Velveteen." In her mind the Velveteen Rabbit and the Easter Bunny seemed to merge.

Also significant was the fact that we were traveling to Granny and Pa's for Easter. This also helped to increase the notion that this was a special time. In fact, the day before we left when Sara decided that she was going to be the Easter Bunny she stated that she needed to "practice being the Easter Bunny" and thus Holy Thursday found her dressed up with bunny mask delivering Easter eggs to our closest neighbors.

One of two points of orchestration on my part was when Sara asked what could she put on cards for everyone, I suggested that because Easter was about Jesus and the Easter Bunny she might draw something about that. About fourteen "Easter Cards" were made in all. . . all individually!

The program of events on Easter Sunday went something like this:

7 a.m. Sara wakes, looks under her bed to see if the Easter Bunny has come. She finds that "he" has left for her a tiny chocolate chicken and a copy of the book and audio tape of the "Velveteen Rabbit."

7-7:30 a.m. Sara stays in bed and with her father's Walkman, listens to and reads the "Velveteen Rabbit." The toy rabbit is tucked under her arm!

8 a.m. Breakfast. Granny gives Sara some eggs and Sara lets Granny in on the fact that she intends to be the Easter Bunny at lunch. But this is their secret!

8:30 a.m. A poster is made for the front door announcing the fact that the "Easter Bunny is coming today." Balloons needed to be blown up as well.

9:30 a.m. I say that I am going to Mass and ask if Sara is coming. She asks me "Why are you going?" I say "To say thanks to God that Jesus 'came alive again'." Sara says that she is coming too.

10 a.m. Mass

11-1 p.m. Sara prepares with Granny. She helps set the table for lunch. She also expresses a wish for some flowers on the table and asks Granny for two vases. When Granny produced the vases Sara wanted to know where they came from. The element of storytelling was fascinating here as Granny explained the aunts who gave them to her when she was a little girl etc. This led to further explanations of the origins of other things in the dining room.

I suggested that Sara might like to put her bunny on the table as well but she would not hear of it. My second attempt at orchestration failed!

1 p.m. Lunch. After the first course, Sara asks if "it is time now?" and I said "I think so." She disappears and reappears with a bunny mask and an overflowing basket of Easter Eggs. She hops around the table placing an egg at each person's place. People called out, "Bunny, over here. My turn. . . may I have another, bunny? You must have been very busy today, bunny?"

1:45 p.m. I rose and called everyone to order. I made a special speech to the Easter Bunny for all the trouble she had gone to, to give us such a happy lunch and so much joy. Everyone clapped and cheered.

7:30 p.m. When Sara was going to bed I prayed with her "Dear Lord, thank you for giving us such a precious child as Sara. She was a wonderful Easter Bunny today." Sara prayed "Dear God, it was great being the Easter Bunny. Thank you that I did it so good."

Some elements of evaluation have already been expressed in the speech of thanks and the evening prayer. On Easter Sunday night, my husband's brother phoned up and requested to speak with Sara. He told her that he had forgotten to take home his little Easter card which Sara had made. Sara said she would post it to him—Pa helped her address the envelope etc. Who knows if that card could have produced an element of transition, change or maybe it was simply something nice that Sara made. . . who knows?

The next day on the journey home, Sara asked us what we liked best about her being the Easter Bunny.
Dad: "Seeing you as the Easter Bunny."
Mum: "Seeing you make everyone so happy."
Sara: "I liked it best when everyone cheered me."

Sara is given a framework by her kindergarten teachers and her family, especially by her mother. But note how the child wants to do it her way, and is rewarded by the esteem she harvests for what she has done. Planners must always be flexible enough to allow the celebrants of ritual to do it their way.

Flexible planning should obviously be behind moves into religious anti-structure. This enterprise is an even more difficult one than the promotion of communitas. How does one help people contact the mystery of God? One approach is to prepare them as far as one can and then set up the support systems for them to spend time in solitude. Whether this "vision quest" is successful or not is left to the individual to assess either alone or preferably in discussion with a spiritual director. [2] This approach is an honest one.

Dealing with emotion

Less honest are assaults on the emotions in highly theatrical liturgies or religious rituals. I have in mind such rituals as reconciliation rites which include appeals to fear or guilt, soft lights and lots of pressure for participants to confess, sometimes publicly, to their "sins." Such a ritual is an invasion of privacy and a sin against liberty. It also uses emotions in an unhealthy way. The ritual exists, it seems, not for the sake of the participants but for the glory of the "performer" who directs it. So the issue is not "Were people helped?" It is "Did the ritual I directed get a measurable response? If so, am I satisfied with the results?" Religious anti-structure, some form of contact with God, is beyond measurement or assessment of this sort. It is between the person and God. As Narelle Mullins commented concerning a possible transition in Sara's self-consciousness, "who knows?" Facilitators can provide opportunities for something to happen, but they are not responsible for it happening. Their job is to set things up, and then get out of the way.

The unhealthy use of emotions needs further explanation. I have no problem with allowing emotions to be expressed. In fact it worries me that rituals which give even the smallest opportunity for emotional release seem to bring an overreaction, particularly among adolescents and young adults. Is it that there are so few chances for emotional release in Western societies? Perhaps we need more, not less, expression of what we feel. But it is unhealthy when someone else tells me what I should feel; this is exploitation. It happens when only one side of an issue is presented, or when "the only possible interpretation" of a complex symbol is given. Such part truths can rouse unwarranted fear and guilt which the expert exploiter can work on. Some religious educators applaud this form of exploitation as being for a good cause. Feelings of fear and guilt can lead to repentance! But exploitation is never a good thing. And how long will the repentance last?

It can be unhealthy, too, when emotions are stirred and released, but no follow-up takes place. This can happen in camps sponsored by religious educators whether communitas or religious anti-structure receives the emphasis. Young people—older primary children, adolescents or young adults from high school or even from college or university—typically go slightly crazy in such situations. They are taken out of their usual routine, they get very little sleep, they are encouraged to express their deepest feelings and/or they have experiences of worship that are charged with emotion. This is heady stuff for the young—even for hardened adults. There is going to be a painful let-down unless people are prepared for a return to the real world, and helped in the real world when classes begin again and it's back to the old grind.

Sample Ritual

Peter Green provides a ritual which shows great sensitivity in its invitation to express emotions. Peter explains that he found that one of the children he taught needed to uncork emotions that had been bottled up:

> The ritual which I will describe was developed in response to an interview with the mother of an 11-year-old child whom I teach. Earlier this year, I read to my class the novel *Bridge To Terabithia*, by Katherine Paterson. This is a story in which the reader encounters and shares the grief suffered by the close relatives and friends of a young girl who drowns. As a consequence, my student, "Emma," became very upset whenever she discussed the subject with her parents. The parents eventually traced Emma's behavior to the death of her maternal grandfather two years previously. Two facts emerged from my initial interview with Emma's parents:
>
> (i) Emma had not been given the opportunity to complete her "grief work" because her parents had not recognised her ability to understand the concept of death.
>
> (ii) The whole family, especially the mother, had not come to terms with the death; e.g. Emma's mother told me that she herself avoids looking at the photograph of her father on the mantelpiece at home, because she knows that it would upset her to do so.
>
> For this family, the funeral Mass and burial had not met their *present* needs, i.e., two years after the death; what they needed was some ritual in which they could externalize and complete their grief. The grief which each family member had suffered privately for two years had to be shared.

Peter went on to design a ritual which could be used by the family. I shall give below the steps Peter suggested, including resources Peter had at hand. The list is clearly a suggested one only, and religious educators can take ideas from it as suits them:

DESCRIPTION OF THE RITUAL

Step 1 : Story
A member of the family reads out the story *When Grandpa*

Died (by Stevens, Margaret, Chicago: Children's Press, 1979).
Discuss.

Step 2 : Sharing feelings
Each member of the family is encouraged to write his/her
own feelings about the deceased. Use these written responses
as a basis for an honest talk about the deceased person.
Allow people to express both positive and negative feelings.

Step 3 : Analyzing feelings
What reactions to death can you imagine? Identify the
different emotions that family members have experienced.
Each person writes his/her reaction to the death. Encourage
people to share their reactions with the family.

Step 4: Healing Service
Having identified such reactions to grief as denial, panic,
anger, depression and guilt, the family members will
participate in a healing service.
Begin by discussing the qualities of oil, e.g. it can supply
heat, light, strength, comfort, healing, power, ease in
movement etc.
Family members will use oil to anoint one another as a sign
of healing of the bitter feelings that they have experienced
since the death of their loved one. The anointing is done on
each person's forehead, in the form of a cross. Explain that
the cross is an action which expresses our love of Christ for
sacrificing his own life for our sake. Each anointing action is
accompanied by the words: "(Name), may the Lord heal you
from the hurt that you have suffered. In the name of the
Father. . ."

Step 5: Writing a letter
Read the story *Dear Nana* (by Taylor, Kaylyn, Melbourne:
Collins/Dove, 1987). Each person is then encouraged to write
a letter to the deceased person. This letter remains
confidential, and will be used later in the ritual.

Step 6: Filmstrips
Discuss the notion of death as a normal, natural part of the

cycle of all living things. Follow this up with filmstrips (such as *Grandpa and Jimmy* and *The Dragonfly*). Discuss feelings, memories and the idea that death is not the end but the beginning of a new life.

Step 7: Prayer

Darken the room, and have family members seated comfortably around a lighted candle placed in the center of the room. Tell the family that they are about to go on a journey to Heaven. Discuss the symbol of the lighted candle, i.e. the light of Christ, the warmth of God's love etc.

Use a "Heaven Meditation" which you have devised to take the family members on a journey to Heaven.

At the conclusion of the meditation, family members are encouraged to share their "journeys" with one another.

Step 8: Planting a Tree

It may be necessary to delete, delay or modify this step of the ritual if, given the circumstances, it is not feasible to grow a plant from seed.

The ritual concludes with the planting of a tree. Preferably, the tree should be a quick-growing deciduous tree which can be grown from seed. The way in which the seed must "die" before rising to a new form of life, as well as the deciduous nature of the tree, can be explored in relation to the theme of death as being necessary in order to rise to new life with God.

A need for reflection on structure

I would like to get back to the discussion of "special times" of retreat or camp which many educational institutions with religious bias have introduced into their programs, and to suggest a simple purpose for them. I propose that the focus be on communitas, helping people communicate person to person. What about prayer, felt contact with God etc? There should be room for prayer, but I would not stress religious anti-structure if my pitch were to the general student body or to a class group or year group. Few students may be at the stage of readiness for all forms of religious experience. If we are going to stress prayer, closeness to God or meditation this should be made clear and the retreat made optional. Some students are open to religious anti-structure, others are not, at least not yet. Individual differences have been recognized for decades in reading and mathematics. It's about time we recognized them in religious education.

Life in today's world is pressured, even for young students. There are so many deadlines, so many things happening that the daily whirl tends to sweep people along without real control. There is little time for reflection, for looking at where we are going, for assessing where we have been. "Special times" ought to be devoted to just such reflection. They should be times when we "get our heads together."

It may seem paradoxical, but I suggest that they should be about reflecting on structure. The communitas of school camps or retreats should be achieved by, first, reflecting on ordinary life as it is lived, its values and its lack of values, and, secondly, by sharing these reflections. The reflection can take place at a number of levels: How do we relate to one another? Is this how we want to relate? What of the school? How do teachers treat students? How do students treat teachers? What is the school about? Competition? Care for others? What?

These are very basic questions. They need asking and they need discussion in most educational institutions. When people honestly discuss such questions they are in communitas. The aim is not, though, to feel affection and support. These may, and should, be expressed, but the principal aim is to question structure. This is a laid-back way of grinding structure down so that it can be built again in different, and more service-oriented, shapes. There is no need to worry about bringing people down from an emotional high as it is hardly likely they will climb there. The realism to be injected will address feelings, to be sure. But these feelings are likely to be expressed in the business of discussing what people see as important in everyday life. They are dealt with on the spot, provided those facilitating the discussions are skilled in such work.

There is work to be done when the special time is over. How can the ideals of the retreat or camp be put into practice? It helps if all those affected by such ideals are present at the discussions. Even if they are not, a golden rule is that practical recommendations be taken out of the liminal time for application to structured time. And these recommendations must be acted on.

There is room for prayer in the process I have outlined: prayer for insight, for help, reflection on life and comparison of life with Gospel ideals. The emphasis is not, however, on felt contact with God. This form of anti-structure is not highlighted. There is a place and a time for religious anti-structure, but in general, it is not for all. It is for some, and should be encouraged for those who are ready for it. For most, the emphasis should be on reflection and discussion about the ordinary. This shared reflection on ordinary life is the principal item I would put on any retreat or camp program for the young. It is, in fact, the item with which most lay people of any age need to deal.

It seems that lay people, in general, do not have time for the essential business of reflecting on life. Clergy and religious are encouraged and supported in setting aside time for reflection and meditation. Such time is a luxury for most lay people. Their world promises them satisfaction, a buzz, even luxurious ease but as some sort of carrot before the donkey. Most chase the carrot frantically, for themselves or their families. Most survive into old age and wonder if all the chasing was worth the effort. They have time to reflect, at last, and old age can be a blessed time. But the reflection should have come sooner.

Sample Ritual

Patricia Moss uses a simple Advent ritual to help the process of reflection in her family. She argues that Advent marks an end to the year's orientation towards work or study:

> Coming as they do at the beginning of the annual Australian period of liminality—the long summer holidays, in so many ways a typical interstructural situation—the rituals of Advent could be used to much greater advantage as the

culmination of our secular, school-based rites of separation which mark the end of the academic year. Our family enters its own period of liminality, marked by the ongoing rituals of Advent, Christmas, New Year, and going away. Much of our regular structure breaks down. Students and workers alike are free of their usual status, free to be themselves. Returning to normal takes place gradually, as Father goes back to work, and we begin back to school preparations. Perhaps Australia Day could be regarded as the final ritual in the reaggregation process, the signal that business as usual is about to resume.

Patricia and her husband, Denis, are aware of the need to reflect through ritual:

Denis and I made a conscious decision in the early years of our marriage to build our own family traditions, because we feel that Australian culture lacks richness and depth. We wanted our children to be aware of their European as well as their Australian heritage, through the appropriation of traditional customs and also by the institution of private family customs to celebrate our own history and sense of community. There are sound psychological reasons too, as children love and need such family traditions which give them a sense of security and family identity.

Advent and Christmas customs form an important part of our family tradition, based on a German/English heritage. My own family background is German Lutheran. While the Advent wreath was not a part of our home life, it was the focal point of our Church worship in the weeks leading up to Christmas. This and the Advent calendar, together with appropriate Bible readings at family prayer time, have become our way of celebrating Advent.

A second reason for developing our Advent ritual centers around a wish to provide a Christian perspective on Christmas—to remind the children by example of the deeper values which lie beyond all the commercial trappings of the Festive Season. For this reason, we keep Advent as a fairly sombre season, akin to Lent, with simple meals, no baking except that which is being stored for Christmas (adding to the anticipation), and delaying the tree and decorations till the last minute.

Patricia and Denis involve their children in preparing the Advent wreath, and organizing the ritual dinner for the first Sunday of Advent:

> The children take charge of preparing the meal, making the wreath, setting the table. Parents help. Status is reversed.

At the end of the meal comes "a symbolic 'letting go'" of the frustrations and worries of the year almost gone. In Patricia's words:

> After the meal comes the more serious side of the ritual. Even so, the structure is quite rudimentary, leaving plenty of space for anti-structure within the general framework. It is Karen's turn to light the candle this year. Denis follows with a reading from Jeremiah 33:14–16. This reading has been selected as suitable for the occasion and simple enough for the younger children to comprehend.
>
> Next comes the symbolic "letting go" of the old year. Each family member is to write on a piece of paper before the meal any hurts, frustrations or worries which have bothered them during the year. These will now be brought forth and burnt in the flame of the candle. Words are not necessary. No script is written. Ritual does not need speech to be meaningful.
>
> Finally, we affirm our support and affection for one another. This year we have decided to follow another old German custom discovered by Mother in her reading. Each person will draw from a hat the name of another family member. Every day of Advent we will attempt to live some of the values of the Christian lifestyle by secretly doing a good turn for that person.
>
> The candle is then extinguished. The ritual is over.

This ritual is a clear attempt to slow down the flow of life a little, to let go of hurts and worries, to gather strength to show concern for others. It promotes reflection, and action consequent on reflection.

Ritual and religious experience

I would like to argue that such reflection can be a form of religious experience. It appears of course to be quite different from religious anti-structure, from being rapt in the felt presence of God. But is it all that different? Let us look a little more closely at these two possible forms of religious experience.

Rudolf Otto is the great expositor of religious anti-structure. His best-known work, *The Idea of the Holy*, begins by laying to one side rational considerations of religion. [3] It is not that Otto wishes to downgrade the importance of the rational. Far from it! But theology has already worked prodigiously at rational description of the attributes of God. The problem is that such a stress on the rational can lead to an error, ". . . the view that the essence of deity can be given completely and exhaustively in such 'rational' attributions." [4]

Otto wishes, then, to move from his own earlier preoccupation with rational theology to an exploration of the nonrational. His book is not about the idea of the Holy: the English version of its title is a complete botch of the German original, *Das Heilige*. Otto wishes, in this book, to look at religious experience as a manifestation of anti-structure, not as an idea.

He finds that the nonrational elements of deity are often expressed in the word "holy," or its equivalents. This word can carry a moral meaning, a holy person being a morally good person. But morality, if seen as "keeping the rules" or "obeying the law", is structure, and clearly the "Holy, Holy, Holy" of Isaiah points beyond structure. There is what Otto calls an "overplus of meaning" in the term, "holy," particularly in its Latin, Greek, and Semitic equivalents. To describe this overplus Otto coins the word, "numinous," from the Latin word for divine power, *numen*. [5]

He goes on to explore the meaning of the numinous. It is Mystery not because we do not know it, but because we cannot know it. By its nature it is beyond our ken, it is "uncanny." Further, it rouses in us feelings of awe and, at the same time, feelings of overpowering love. These emotions are not only psychological states, that is, emotions that rise in us. They are primarily the effect of our contact with the numinous. Schleiermacher's description of the most basic religious experience as a feeling of absolute dependence was, then, mistaken. It did not stress sufficiently that this sense of dependence is not merely subjective but requires "an object outside the self." This object is the numinous, the mystery which excites both awe and fascination. [6]

For Otto, a person's religious experience is a shadow cast by the presence of the mighty rock, the numinous. Otto goes on to formulate his classic definition of the numinous: *Mysterium tremendum et fascinans.* Religious experience is contact with the numinous in the sense that the divine power, the "numen," must be experienced as present:

> There must be felt a something "numinous," something bearing the character of a "numen," to which the mind turns spontaneously. [7]

Religious experience is often something dramatic. Otto cites Abraham's contact with God before the destruction of Sodom. But the experience can be a far more gentle thing.

> The feeling of it may at times come
> sweeping like a gentle tide, pervading
> the mind with a tranquil mood of deepest
> worship. It may pass over into a more
> set and lasting attitude of the soul,
> continuing, as it were, thrillingly
> vibrant and resonant, until at last it
> dies away and the soul resumes its
> "profane," nonreligious mood of
> everyday experience. [8]

The point stressed here is not whether experience of the numinous is dramatic or not, but that it does not belong, in Otto's view, to ordinary life. Religious experience, for Otto, is reserved to those times when we feel the presence of the numinous. These are not ordinary times, but extraordinary. Religious experience is for the privileged moments when we move out of profane existence, out of our usual non-religious world.

Otto's theories about religious experience seem far away from the practical business of religious education. But they provide a model for contact with the divine which surfaces again and again. The old-fashioned ways of teaching children to pray often took the form of parent saying to child, "Now, Johnny, kneel down, close your eyes and say 'Dear God'. . ." Johnny often raised all sorts of theological problems by asking God to bless his dog as well as his parents and family. But the basic approach of the parent was, and often still is, an Otto one. The child is told to kneel in awe before the numinous, close out the profane world and try to contact God.

Many religious educators feel that retreats or camps should be about leaving the world behind to find God. Here the move from the structures of everyday into liminality has, as its purpose, the hope that people will contact the numinous in some direct way. Some religious educators may feel guilty if they don't try for this contact, or encourage their students to try for it. I know many very good people who have tried and experienced nothing, no dramatic apparitions and not even a "gentle tide. . . of deepest worship." "Aridity," the classic word for not experiencing anything even in the liminal situation, presents a problem only when guilt arises as a consequence.

The Otto model of religious experience should not be presumed to be the only model; it is *not* the only possible model. However, there is nothing wrong with this approach. People may move away from structure into liminality, there to meet God. Generations of hermits and anchorites did precisely that, and today's communities of contemplatives are doing the same thing.

Some excellent research indicates that the Otto form of religious experience may be far more relevant to the world outside monasteries than we think. The Religious Experience Research Unit at Oxford has been foremost in this work. [9] Such investigators as Edward Robinson, retired director of the unit, and its present director, David Hay, hint that established religion may be losing its nerve by not dealing with the body of evidence that points to direct experience of the numinous among, perhaps, one third of the population. Both their research and the strategy it seems to imply deserve careful attention. But again, the point is that Otto's direct experience of the numinous is not the only form of religious experience. It may occur in some lives, but it seems to happen rarely even in these lives. In many other lives, it does not happen at all.

An alternative notion of religious experience

There is another notion of "religious" which needs exploring if an alternative notion of "religious experience" is to be developed. John Shea's work, already alluded to, hints at it. For Shea, I find my religious identity, who I am in the last analysis, by telling and retelling "my story." [10] As I focus on the significant events of my life and recount them over and over I form my ideology. I know who I am, and what I believe in. Shea, the master story-teller, readily agrees that the stories of the Gospels will probably be highly relevant to my life. They can help me interpret my own story. But my story is the important one for me.

The real me stands up as I crawl out from behind the roles and status of structure. I find my religious identity by finding out who I really am, and I can do this by reflecting on my life and expressing what I feel in the sort of simple ritual the Moss family use at the beginning of Advent.

This finding of the real self is religious, for Shea. He does not, to my knowledge, spell out the theology behind his assertion. My guess is that his theological justification lies somewhere in the developing area of the theology of revelation. Revelation was once regarded as belonging to scripture: God's complete revelation was in Christ, fulfilling the partial revelations of the Old Testament. Then creation became a locus for revelation: God's first word to us was the world God created for us to live in. Now the focus seems to have moved to contemporary living: God's first word to me is my life. God speaks to me first in the events of daily living, in the words and challenges which friends and enemies direct at me, and in the moods and questions which seem to drift into my days. [11]

In this sort of thinking there is no compartmentalizing of life into sacred and profane. God's revelation is not reserved to special moments when the numinous breaks into my life and I react in awe and fascination. Rather, God's revelation to me can and does take place in the most mundane of events. The trick is to recognize that these events are not mundane. That the ordinary is never ordinary if only I am awake to what it reveals.

Gabriel Moran, a writer who has consistently and painstakingly explored the notion of revelation, puts the matter well. Arguing for the usefulness of the term "religious development" he insists that human development must be religious in the sense that:

> A beginning way to define the word
> religious would be to say that it
> refers to whatever keeps open the
> process of development. [12]

Human development, of its very nature, is religious for Moran. If true development, or growth, or progress happens—the term used does not matter—then we are dealing with a religious phenomenon. God is present, and a human person is responding positively to God's presence.

Moran goes on to give a fuller, though still preliminary meaning to the adjective, "religious." It:

> ... refers to those attitudes and activities that challenge the
> limits of experience. In this sense "religious experience" is
> not a set of experiences (in contrast to non-religious
> experiences), nor is religious language a particular set of
> words or statements. Rather, the adjective involves an
> intended redundancy, not a reference to a particular set of
> experiences but to all of experience. The word religious
> should remind us that experience always includes more than
> we have grasped. When we think we have exhausted the
> resources of language, then religious use of language protests
> against prematurely stopping with the world as it is
> ordinarily named. [13]

Moran, like Otto, points to a reality beyond the ordinary: "experience always includes more than we have grasped." But this something more is not found by going apart from the ordinary, but by exploring its depths. If we go deep enough into the ordinary, we find God, we are in the area of the religious. This area is marked by a refusal to stop prematurely with the world "as it is ordinarily named." The religious person refuses to name people as "useless" even if they are manifestly imperfect in mind or body. Religious language looks again at "failure," at "unimportant," at "ordinary."

Moran's perceptive exploration of the term, "religious," supports
the proposal that religious experience need not involve felt contact
with the numinous. That is, religious experience is not necessarily
a set of extraordinary experiences. Experience, all of experience,
can be religious, if it is perceived as including "more than we have
grasped." This quality of perception is not, of course, easy to come
by. This is why it is absolutely necessary that all who want to find
God, especially lay people, be given time for reflection. This time
can be a "flight from the world."

It will be more helpful, and healthy, if it is used for reflection on
ordinary living. This means the reassessment of the usual structures,
a questioning of the roles and expectations that govern lives. It
means that structures will be treated not as ends in themselves or
as the powerful tyrants of life, but as servants of life open to other
human beings and to God. People need time to pull out of the usual
rat-race so that they can see the rat-race for what it is and go back
in there to change it or, at least, not be destroyed by it.

Some of the thinking that could be behind the planning of a
retreat or camp has been outlined, and options set out for religious
educators. Turner provides the framework: structure or anti-
structure and, if the latter, what type? One viable option would be
to encourage open, honest discussion of the normal structures of
life, with a move into communitas, not for the warm feelings this
brings, but for the changes in future living it could bring. There
will be warmth, but also hurt and wounded egos, and, hopefully,
healing if changes are to be agreed to and worked for. This could,
of course, be a recommendation not only for retreats and camps
but also for all of religious education. It makes a good general aim,
although there will be times when working away at the evaluation
of ordinary living is not the need of this group at this moment.

As I have suggested, there will be some who want to go aside to
meet God in a special way before they come back into the affairs
of daily living. Religious educators have to recognize this need.
They may not be able to meet it. They need, then, to call on expert
spiritual directors for help. Spiritual direction seems to be a
growth industry in religious education. [14] And well it might be. It
is one way of recognizing that some people have special needs
which may take them outside the expertise of the general
practitioner in religious education.

There are other times where those being educated need to work solidly on their own life stories. Before they share, they need to remember. Journal keeping or creative writing techniques that open the past could be the techniques used.

Still another set of needs is tied to religious traditions. If Shea is right, many of us can understand our own stories better if we listen to the "stories" of our religious tradition. The answers the tradition provides come as answers to questions we are asking. There can be a sense of recognition when we listen to the tradition: "Yes, I know that is right. It makes sense when I think of the things I've been trying to work out." We are back in the interpretation of daily living, but studying the content of tradition can, and should, have relevance for this.

Religious education involves many strategies, then. My point is that educators should plan which of these strategies to use with a given group at a given time. The structure/anti-structure framework can help this planning.

Planning for ritual—the nonliturgical

Let me turn, finally, to the practical use of ritual in religious education. I have already dropped plenty of general hints about this. Ritual involves the use of symbols to express meaning. It is a powerful tool to help us express what we feel and to allow us to explore feelings which we cannot even acknowledge in other ways. But how does it fit into the planning religious educators must do? How does the structure/anti-structure distinction help in this planning?

One response is to "leave it to the clergy." If the local pastor or one of his assistants is good at liturgy, the problem is solved. Or is it? The answer, of course, is "No!" Ritual is not always liturgy. To restrict all religious ritual to the official liturgy of the Church is educational nonsense. All religious educators must learn to use ritual as normal procedure in religious education. It must not be equated with the Eucharist and the other sacraments. Further, religious educators who do not happen to be ordained should stop passing the buck to the clergy. There may be some parishes where the liturgy does not help religious education, but this does not prevent teachers and other religious educators from planning nonliturgical rituals.

Sample Ritual

One such ritual is outlined below. Pat Spannagle designed it with her Year Four class. It is a "bread and butter" paraliturgy, obviously fitting into a unit of classroom work. A priest is involved, but need not have been.

I designed the ritual as the culmination paraliturgy after a series of lessons on reconciliation. The *first* of these lessons was the *scripture story* of Moses receiving the ten commandments. Then the retelling in Jesus' words of N.T. God's Law of Love. We then *related* the fifth commandment "care for others" to our 1988 *playground experience*.

The *second* lesson was one on *reconciliation;* the need for forgiveness and being able to forgive. We discussed the ripple effect on class *community* and for communal reconciliation.

The *third* lesson was on the meaning of *symbols*. I asked the children to bring one symbol each that meant something to them and explain it to the class. There were symbols of "brokenness" and symbols of "wholeness." From this I discovered what symbols were meaningful to the children. We also discussed traditional Church symbols that made them feel good. I had observed already that our normal morning prayer ritual became more reflective when we prayed with candles and flowers.

The *fourth* lesson was on prayer. I wanted the children to write their own prayer of sorrow which would include meaningful language for them.

The *fifth* lesson was the reading and dramatisation of the Prodigal Son. This class becomes totally involved in, enjoys and is good at dramatisation. Drama also helps to interiorize values.

In the *last* lesson we put all the elements of the ritual together, in order. For the class to partake with total involvement, they needed to know and feel confident in every part of the ritual. Ritual is repetitive, so we practised our ritual.

It will be seen from this that I *consulted* with my students. I also consulted the Religious Education Co-ordinator, Parish Priest and various school paraliturgy resources for practical help on structure, language and symbols.

RECONCILIATION PARALITURGY YEAR 4

Opening Hymn: They'll know we are Christians
Children process into Church. Each child carries their own symbol of "brokenness". . . e.g. broken toy, torn magazine, bandaged knee, hurt feelings.
One child carries the Bible, which is then placed on the lectern.
Children sit in small groups "broken up."

Religious Education Co-ordinator: We have come together today to learn God's Law of Love and to remember how we care for others. When we hurt others we hurt ourselves and we hurt God. Our class is not happy when children are hurting.

Each group tells of experience (summarised and in known prayer form).

Group 1: We did not care for others when we broke these toys.
We are sorry, God.

Group 2: We did not care for others when we damaged these books and magazines.
We are sorry, God.

Group 3: We did not care for others when we mistreated flowers, plants, trees and other living things of nature.
We are sorry, God.

Group 4: We did not care for others when we punched and
kicked and had fights.
We are sorry, God.

Group 5: We did not care for others when we teased and
called names and whispered behind others' backs.
We are sorry, God.

Children then move into large groups to listen to the Word of
God.

Reading: Lk.15:11-24 The Lost Son

Two children share reading and two children dramatise the
story.

At end of reading all reflect for a short time.

Priest: What is Jesus telling us in the story?
What does it mean for us today?
How can this help our class?
Do you know the great Law of Love that God has
given us?
Let us say it together.

Children now take unlit candle and move to Priest with
Paschal Candle (lit). Priest lights each child's candle from the
Paschal Candle.

Each child responds as he/she is handed the candle: "Jesus
is with me. I can be like Him."

Then child moves to stand in a circle around the Paschal
Candle. When last child has joined the circle, all reflect for a
short while on caring for others and reconciling with those
we have hurt.

Virginia Hine argues, in a rich article "Self-Generated Ritual:
Trend or Fad?," that there is a need for ritual in Western civilization.
She goes on,

This need could express itself either in
a revitalization of traditional
rituals or as an eruption of innovative
new forms of archetypal ritual processes. [15]

Religious educators should drop Hine's "either/or" model. There is a need both to revitalize traditional (liturgical) rituals, and to develop new nonliturgical rituals. This two-pronged need should form the basis for planning the use of ritual in religious education.

The glory, and the weakness, of official liturgy is that it carries the deepest meanings a community can give to religion. These meanings are of the very essence of people's lives and, as such, they are often taken for granted. But self-generated ritual requires us to reflect. What do we really feel about *this* death, *this* birth, *this* homecoming, *this* going away? Ritual grows naturally out of reflection, it articulates what reflection gropes towards. It helps us to say who we are at this moment, in this web of circumstances.

The subject of Hine's article, self-generated rituals, are the nontraditional, nonliturgical rituals that require creativity-based-on-reflection to develop. They will be gimmicks, part of a fad that quickly passes if they respond to the question: What's new that we can try? They will be part of a healthy trend if they are developed to express something that needs expressing.

Jan Kelly found that the Year Three classes in her school shared a number of fears:

Year Three in the primary school marks the end of an important stage in the physical, social and emotional development of a young child. Many basic skills have been mastered, sincere friends have been made and many attitudes and values formed that will permeate their entire school lives. This year in Grade Three has seen the introduction and development of the whole language approach. For the teacher it has been a year of adjustment to a different approach to teaching, of growth with the children in a less rigid, freer school day, of learning, along with them, to communicate with each other, to express our feelings, to have fun while learning in new and different ways.

In the course of the whole language approach, the children have expressed many of the concerns and fears they have for the future. Many of these fears are associated with promotion to Year Four, to the "big school," which involves many roles with which the children are unfamiliar—different playgrounds and duties, participation in athletic and swimming events, sacramental preparation. An additional survey carried out by the class teachers on "Next Year— Grade Four" revealed a variety of fears:

1. separation from friends
2. inability to cope with the work
3. trying new and different activities
4. homework
5. the treatment meted out by some children when one shows pride in achievement
6. teachers who are loud and rough (Year Four is usually the first year these youngsters encounter a male teacher!)

A "big book" made by the teacher to help express some of these fears has been very popular with the children in shared reading time, where they are encouraged to share and discuss any book or magazine in the classroom.

Jan went on to develop, with other teachers and with the children, a ritual for the last day of the Year Threes' time together. The teachers of Year Four were part of the process, too, and began to plan a welcoming ritual for the next year.

Jan's ritual allowed time for the articulation of memories of the past, and of fears for the future. It ended with a stress on hope and achievement. Each child was given a "mini-merit," which Jan explains:

In the past, merit awards were presented monthly at assembly for various achievements in each of the classes. Not all children would receive a merit award. Mini-merits are presented to *every* child to symbolize some achievement of which the individual can be proud. These are the gifts we have been given and for these we give thanks and praise to God.

Jan and her colleagues are not in the business of gimmicks here. They have recognized fears which children in their school have, and they have designed a ritual to address these fears. Their ritual expresses values which help children. The ritual affirms, and this affirmation was needed.

Self-generated rituals

The first step in introducing such rituals to a school or parish is to develop a climate of ritual. Religious educators and those they educate should be imbued with the spirit that anything can be ritualized. This is not easy to bring about. I remember one college where a creative arts teacher took on the task almost single-handedly by stirring up enthusiasm for a series of "fun" celebrations. It has to start somewhere.

It may start with structure: say a number of religious or nonreligious occasions where something to be celebrated is imposed on those celebrating. "Let's do. . ." may sound relaxed enough, but people know when they are being organized. The ideal, however, involves people recognizing that they have a need to ritualize, and getting together to prepare the ritual. More often than not the religious educator will need to point out the need and will preside over the preparation of the ritual. Ideals are seldom realized, at least in the early stages.

Again, the religious educator needs to ask the question about where to put the emphasis: on structure or on anti-structure? If structure is the aspect which predominates the educator may need to organize blatantly—pleasantly, but blatantly. If anti-structure is the value to be stressed, organization must be at a minimum. The educator must leave the role of structure figure as quickly and completely as possible. The group who participate in the ritual must plan it. They must be left free to express what they want to express. They may consult the educator as one whom they trust or as one who has certain skills.

Here the educator is moving away from the role of official educator and becoming a member of the group rather than its organizing leader. Remember the way Narelle encouraged her daughter, but also allowed her freedom. Jan actively helped her class to articulate fears they perhaps could not put into words at first. There is a delicate balance between promotion and manipulation. These two educators promote ritual, but do not manipulate children into performing it. Their children ritualize something they (the children) wish to ritualize.

Let me give some examples of nonliturgical rituals which can be self-generated. One I know of began with a high school teacher. He suggested to a group of students that one of the activities of the "pastoral time" scheduled on the school program could be prayer. What if, each week, one or two members of the group took responsibility for leading group prayer? The idea caught on and the group prays in its own way. The students choose the records, the poems, the readings. . . whatever they feel can help prayer.

What began as a suggestion from a structure person seems to have led to self-generated ritual. It is not liturgical. At times it may be paraliturgical in the sense that scripture readings are highlighted. But the label does not matter if there is movement into prayer which the group owns.

Virginia Hine gives examples of rituals which developed from strongly felt needs. She writes of a high school graduation class which rejected the official graduation ceremony as meaningless. They went through it for the sake of their parents, but really wanted an alternative ritual. They asked for help, but the rite of passage they celebrated was their ritual.

She writes, too, of her own need to ritualize her grief at her husband's death. She had been through the normal grieving process at his funeral, but Western societies have gradually tried to speed up grief. A wife who has shared decades of living with her husband is really expected to forget grief and get on with life within a week or so. Hine knew intuitively that this was wrong:

> In my own experience of widowhood,
> I found an unexpected but deep need to
> terminate the mourning period in some
> external fashion. It was three and a
> half years before I was ready, but when
> I was ready it became imperative to
> ritualize the change. [16]

She took her husband's ashes to the Bahamas, where they had sailed together. After a long preparation, involving fasting and thinking over what she was about, she rowed out from the shore and dropped her husband's ashes, and a clay effigy of herself into the water. One part of life was officially over; the grief had been closed off.

This was clearly a private ritual generated out of a deep personal need. Hine records that the Bahamian people in the small out-island town where she stayed understood what she was doing, and supported her by organizing a ritual of farewell to her husband and insisting that she join them. She was fortunate to find this community support but that, too, was an important part of her experience.

Other farewells can generate rituals with something of the rich investment of Hine's end of grieving. A group of people who are about to separate have often shared much together. Their going apart can be marked by a formal celebration, with the emotion kept to the last hugs and tears. It is better if people say good-bye more expansively, if they take time to remember, and to break open what they have shared. This process can be ritualized in all sorts of imaginative ways.

I remember one group of college students who were about to graduate organizing their own "M.A.S.H. bash," based on the final good-bye episode of the TV series. But simple dominant symbols, such as a photograph album, can serve as foci for the memory sharing that cries out to happen.

Sample Ritual

When my own mother died, I went back to the city where she, and I, had been born. She had lived there all her life and wanted to be buried in the same grave as her husband. Her funeral was a great family ritual. But I felt dissatisfied. She had visited my home every summer for years before her death and had many friends in the city where I lived. I wanted to include them in the mourning process. So I generated a ritual for all who had known Annie during her summer visits.

The dominant symbols were simple: small pebbles and a crystal salad bowl. The bowl was a beautiful thing. It had belonged to my mother ever since I could remember. It may even have been one of her wedding gifts. The action of the ritual was that each person placed a pebble in the bowl while telling of some memory of

Annie. I told people that I would take the pebbles and place them on Annie's grave the next time I was able to visit it.

We had set the atmosphere with music and candle light, and the ritual seemed to "work." People did share their memories, helped by the simple ritual of placing these pebbles in a bowl. Of course, both pebbles and bowl were imbued with strong meaning in this ritual. The symbols were simple enough, but rich in significance. I had organized them, all the same. In a sense I imposed them on the group. The freedom of anti-structure came in the unpressured time allowed for memory-sharing.

The development of self-generated ritual may mark an important step forward in education. In the religious sphere I have seen it touch areas where official liturgy has little, if anything, to say. Helping parents express their grief after miscarriage is one such. [17] I have heard of other parents who have designed rituals which directly parallel parish liturgy, such as baptism of their own children. I can understand that these particular parents feel that baptism, administered by them, is far more meaningful than the ritual their local church offers. It is a pity they feel this way, and even more of a pity if their feelings are fully justified.

The general strategy I wish to offer here is not, however, offered as a replacement for official liturgy. I repeat that religious educators need to work at developing nonliturgical ritual *and* to work at improving liturgical worship. There will be times when liturgy will be so poorly done in a parish that other rituals seem to supply what is lacking. This is obviously not an ideal situation. Nonliturgical ritual should not take its justification from it. Rather, nonliturgical rituals should accompany a strong liturgical worship. Clearly, the two forms of ritual are symbiotic; each gives life to the other and supports it. Nonliturgical rituals help people express meaning which liturgy does not touch. This is its real justification. The liturgy cannot be expected to express every meaning in life. It is ridiculous to move into formal worship every time we want to say good-bye, or congratulate someone, or pray, even if we want to do these things in a religiously oriented school or parish.

Nonreligious rituals, particularly if they are generated out of a need to express meaning, are the stuff of everyday life. They create a readiness for ritual which is important in itself, and which also helps liturgy to thrive. Religious educators who wish to encourage meaningful liturgical worship could adopt, as their first strategy, the development of nonliturgical rituals among those they educate.

Liturgical ritual

The second, the inevitable strategy, will, of course, deal directly with liturgy. What can religious educators do about this? One answer would be to say that it depends on the role of the religious educator: the clergy must deal directly with the problem, other religious educators can, at best, support the clergy, or, at worst, get on with rituals which do not need clergy. This is another version of passing the buck. It is no answer at all if the liturgy is understood as the work of the whole community realizing itself. [18] All religious educators must be involved in dealing directly with the liturgy.

The distinction between structure and anti-structure again provides a useful framework. What is the emphasis a parish is seeking in each liturgical act it performs? This, of course, is quite a question to put to a parish. Professional religious educators who have put in the effort to read even a small book such as this can see the value in applying theory in practical religious education. But is it possible to put such a theoretical framework before a whole parish?

Strategy

One attempt I have made at it follows. I had been invited to a parish to help introduce the Rite of Christian Initiation of Adults (R.C.I.A.) program. The principal of the parish school called in the debts I owed him, so I agreed. The general brief was to get people thinking about what baptism involved. I decided to use anthropological theory. Were unbaptized adults being called to join structure or anti-structure? Were they being invited to join a club with strict rules of membership with club fees and with an already established hierarchy of officials (structure)? Or was the invitation coming from a group who were more like a family, who would welcome newcomers with warmth and be open to the richness the newcomers could bring (anti-structure)? Of course, a parish has something of both models, but where did this parish wish to put the emphasis?

Below are a number of things you might like to bring into your life. Consider them as possible New Year resolutions.
A. Read them, then put their numbers under

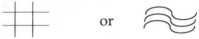

where ▦ represents straight-line living, an organized life-style etc, while 〰 is more relaxed. . .

1. I would like to be on time for everything.
2. I would like to be peaceful inside.
3. I would like to take time to look at the flowers I grow.
4. I would like to read more.
5. I would like to enjoy a good party every now and then.
6. I would like to keep my next door neighbor on side.
7. I would like to be better trained at my job.
8. I would like to learn something cultural (like pottery or wood-carving).
9. I would like to go for picnics with my family.
10. I would like to really listen when other people speak to me.
11. I would like to make sure my kids do their homework.
12. I would like to keep some time for myself each day.
13. I would like to share a good bottle of wine with my (wife, husband, friends) occasionally.
14. I would like to wear fashionable clothes.
15. I would like to be more careful of my diet.
16. I would like to show more respect for my boss.
17. I would like to do something I really like doing every now and then.
18. I would like to treat everyone in my life fairly.

Circle *your* first five priorities in the eighteen items.
B. Suppose Jesus were alive today and were living the same sort of life as you are living. Tick what you think would be *his* first five priorities in the above list.
How many of these fit under ▦ ? How many under 〰 ? Any comment?

I felt that I could not decide for them. I knew that anti-structure would sound more attractive to most, unless the organizing faction was out in force. I decided then to develop an instrument which would be as neutral as possible.

This was the page given to the parish gathering:
(*see opposite page*)

This particular parish opted for the wave-lines of anti-structure rather than the grid of structure. There were several vocal dissenters, folk who thought that, at that time, the emphasis should have been on structure. Clearly, the dialogue had to continue.

The sacraments

The point here is strategy, planning. No matter how it is done, the structure/anti-structure framework can be communicated, and it must be if it is to have value for planning the liturgy. Planners need to ask: is reconciliation about settling one's sins before God's representative, and performing the penance these sins deserve (structure)? Or is it setting out how one is living, including the failures, before a loving God who wants nothing more than to welcome one home (anti-structure)? Where should the emphasis be put in teaching about the sacrament and in preparing sacramental rituals?

Each of the sacraments can be treated in this way. Sometimes this will bring out anomalies. If confirmation introduces our young adults to more active service in the community, where is the evidence of this service? If the anointing of the sick expresses the community's support for the sick person, how is this support shown? The framework helps us get behind our liturgical rhetoric. If we really want communitas, what are we doing about it? If we are doing nothing, liturgical ceremony can be a form of escapism. The link between liturgy and life is not being forged.

EUCHARIST

Finally, let us look at the problem sacrament, the eucharist. Liturgical reform has made real progress in making the other sacraments accessible to people. But reform of the eucharistic celebration still seems a doubtful success. A great deal of effort has gone into encouraging participation in the Sunday liturgy, but many are simply not attending and a constant lament from the young whose parents force them to attend is that the eucharist is boring. The picture varies from parish to parish, and from denomination to denomination. Some great things are being done, but there seems need to do better.

One problem is that structure does have a stranglehold on many Sunday liturgies. It is no small organizational feat to move hundreds of people in and out of a building on the hour each Sunday morning. The show must be over on time to let the people out and to clear the parking lot for the next congregation. So there is a strong time pressure. This is a great enemy of anti-structure. How can people relax, communicate or pray when the stop watch is on them? They manage, but not well.

Of course, structure has its rightful place. Some Catholic anthropologists, such as Turner and Mary Douglas, have insisted that attendance at Sunday Mass, and similar Catholic rituals, act as "markers" clearly indicating membership of the "Catholic social group." [19] This is true, but surely Christians are looking for more from the eucharist than identification with their particular denomination.

There are two anti-structure values we are looking for: one is communitas, the other a sense of being in God's presence. Let us look at these two as candidates for emphasis at the eucharist.

Communitas is not easy to achieve in parishes where the typical Sunday congregation consists of hundreds of people who barely know one another. To some extent, talk of communitas, communicating as person to person, is so much hot air in such parishes. But it is important to have communitas as an ideal. If we do try for some sense of belonging in a liturgical group it will lead us to certain practicalities: cutting down congregation size where possible, choosing architecture (or seating) which helps people feel that they are together, reserving the Blessed Sacrament in a side chapel so that the people assemble in a meeting place, not in a throne room.

It will lead to a certain style, too. Care will be taken with the welcoming rites. Perhaps this is the time to spell out the parish's living concerns: Mr. . . who is dying in St. Luke's hospital and has recently been anointed, the R.C.I.A. group who are preparing for baptism... (I remember suggesting such a welcome in a parish and being told there was not enough time for it—structure, again!).

There will be care with communication, too. The Liturgy of the Word may be a time for teaching. It may, to use communitas language, be a time for breaking open the Word together. This may mean that people spend time outside the eucharist reading, meditating on, and discussing the readings. It may mean that, inside the eucharist, the readings are explained in such a way that people understand them. I wonder if the readings chosen are not too much for some congregations. We read learned translations from the Hebrew scriptures or Paul which mean little to most people. It may be better to have one reading, and to have time to explain it and to reflect on it.

This last point leads into examination of the second possible focus for the eucharist, a sense of being in God's presence. Have we lost this in the present liturgy? Has our worship become too egalitarian? In the Catholic Mass the mysterious silence of the pre-Vatican II Canon, broken by the bells announcing consecration, and the esoteric and ancient Latin have been replaced by a democratic openness of intent that seems to have destroyed all sense of mystery. [20] In the Anglican tradition, moves away from the cadences of the King James Bible may have done the same thing. To ask whether more has been lost than gained is a fair question. But even if we answer the question in favor of the new, the question of religious anti-structure remains. That is, even if we decide that it is better to have comprehension than mystery, where does God fit in?

It seems we reach out to God by emphasizing our Christian tradition. The concerns we have in this liturgy, the lives we lead now are joined to the death and resurrection of Jesus. We were baptized into his death and resurrection, and in the eucharist we give thanks for it and continue our entry into this "mystery" present again.

It is not appropriate here to develop a whole theology of eucharist. The point is that eucharistic ritual cries out for emphasis on what George Worgul calls the "root metaphor" of Christianity, the death and resurrection of Jesus. [21] The whole environment, the music, the words spoken, the symbols used must emphasize this root metaphor. I have already mentioned the need for avoiding "minimal" symbols. If we must have wafers and brown-yellow wine at communion, at least have real loaves of bread and bottles of red wine clearly visible. This food and drink, broken and poured out, speak to people of the ways in which ordinary life can hold the divine.

The eucharist seems the occasion above all other occasions when we protest against prematurely stopping with the world as it is ordinarily named. The sacrament shouts out that the ordinary things of life have heights and depths beyond our comprehension. It celebrates the sort of "religious experience" which consists in recognizing God's action in the happenings of daily life. Archbishop Hollingworth, the Anglican bishop of Brisbane, is on record concerning the Roman Catholic tradition:

> . . . there is something gutsy about the Roman way of doing things; the profane all mixed up with the sacred. It is an ordinary part of life they celebrate. [22]

This puts it well. For each of us the eucharistic ritual points to this kind of experience. It may not express it, in all its complexity, for each person at each Mass. This is too much to expect. But if the ritual is to make any connection between ordinary life and the action of God, certain moves need to be made.

First, people's ordinary lives need some expression in the liturgy. Their present needs, where their story is up to now, can be expressed at the welcome, in the "prayers of the faithful," or in some other form of public statement in words or symbol. The expression must not be reduced to some general formula, as happens in most "prayers of the faithful," but must genuinely tell something of these human stories.

Second, there must be a clearly recognizable celebration of the presence of Christ's death and resurrection in symbol and act.

Third, people must be helped to put their lives and Christ's saving acts together. This can be done in symbolic actions such as the offertory procession. The celebrant can, and should, highlight the connections. Perhaps most importantly, people should be given time to reflect on the meaning of the symbols they have used and so make connections for themselves. There should be room for each person to apply the communal act to life, to interpret the symbols, to highlight the one or two personal meanings from among the many which each symbol carries.

This space for reflection should be part of most religious rituals. If it is omitted the person is alienated or manipulated. But if each person has the chance to reflect on the richness of symbols and to make the connections between ritual and life, that person can recognize that all experience does truly include more than we can grasp.

Religious educators can bring new life to liturgy if they do the hard work of planning and implementing strategies that help people explore the theological depths of liturgy and apply their explorations to ordinary living. But planning is the key. I suggest a viable set of aims for most parish liturgies would be, first, to create and celebrate a sense of communitas as far as this is possible: and, second, to put people, in all their ordinariness, in touch with the death and resurrection of Jesus. Neither aim is easily achieved, no matter how much theological rhetoric about community and salvation pours out. The ideal Christian worshiping community is not part of the present dispensation. It belongs to the "not yet" of theology. Good planning can help, though, to keep us on the road to the "not yet" and to stop us chasing after what should be "not at all."

Discussion Questions

1. When do you reflect on how you are living your life?
   Do you do this alone, or does talking with others help?

2. Plan and perform a simple ritual based on your reflections on your own life. It can be a private ritual, or a small-group one. Once you have finished the ritual, reflect on it. Would you change anything? What? Why?

3. Try encouraging your family to generate a ritual expressing their values, or hopes, or. . .!

4. How can you improve liturgical rituals in your parish? If you can't change the status quo, think about your personal involvement in the present liturgy. Any possibilities of being a more "active" participant?

Notes
   1. Gelineau, J., *The Liturgy Today and Tomorrow*, translated D.Livingstone, London: Darton, Longman and Todd, 1978, pp.40-42.
   2. Hine, Virginia, "Self-Generated Ritual: Trend or Fad?," *Worship*, 55 (1981), 404-19, especially p.408.
   3. Otto, Rudolf, *The Idea of the Holy*, translated John W. Harvey, New York: Galaxy (O.U.P.), 1964. Original German title, *Das Heilige*, 1917.
   4. *Ibid.*, pp. 1-2.
   5. *Ibid.*, pp. 5-7.
   6. *Ibid.*, pp. 9-11.
   7. *Ibid.*, p.11.
   8. *Ibid.*, p.12.
   9. Robinson, Edward, *The Original Vision*, Oxford: RERU, 1977.
      Hay, David, *Exploring Inner Space*, Harmondsworth: Penguin, 1982.
  10. Shea, John, "Storytelling and Religious Identity," *Chicago Studies*, 21/1 (Spring 1982), 23-43.
  11. For revelation and creation: Latourelle, Rene, *Theologie de la Revelation*, Bruges: Desclee de Brouwer, 1963. For revelation and life: Baum, Gregory, *Man Becoming: God in Secular Language*, New York: Herder and Herder, 1970.
  12. Moran, Gabriel, *Religious Education Development*, Minneapolis, Minnesota: Winston, 1983, p.129.
  13. *Ibid.*, p.130.
  14. Note its popularity in such post-graduate courses as those presented by the Graduate School of Religion and Religious Education of Fordham University, New York.
  15. Hine, Virginia, "Self-Generated Ritual: Trend or Fad?" *Worship*, 55 (1981), 404-19, in particular, p.405.
  16. *Ibid.*, p.412.
  17. See Edmondson, Kate, "The Church: Women and Miscarriage," *Compass Theology Review*, 17/2 (Winter, 1983), 41-3.
  18. Kilmartin, Edward J., "Theology of the Sacraments: Towards a New Understanding of the Chief Rites of the Church of Jesus Christ," in Duffy, R.A. (ed.), *Alternative Futures for Worship I*, Collegeville, MN: The Liturgical Press, 1987, 123-75.
  19. Turner, V., "Ritual, Tribal and Catholic," *Worship*, 50/6 (November, 1976), 504-26.
      Douglas, Mary, *Natural Symbols*, Harmondsworth: Penguin, 1978, Chapter 3.
  20. Flanagan, K., "Ritual Form: Liturgy's Sociological Dimension," *Modern Theology*, 2/4 (July, 1986), 341-61.
  21. Worgul, George S., "The Loss of Imagination and Metaphor: An Impoverished Assembly," *New Catholic World*, November-December, 1982, 276-9.
  22. Quoted in Peterson, Don, "Church Under Challenge," *The Courier-Mail*, 23 December, 1989, pp. 17, 19.

Conclusion

Cultural anthropology can make a useful contribution to religious education. This book has explored the insights of cultural anthropologists, particularly Victor Turner, into ritual and has tried to apply these insights to religious education. It is my experience that religious educators are extremely busy people. It may be useful, then, to end with a check-list of recommendations. You have read the book, now what practical resolutions can you draw? How can you translate this theory into everyday practice?

First, to repeat a warning! The terminology used in this book comes from cultural anthropology. It may not be appropriate in religious education. Even the basic term, "ritual", may cause problems in a parish or classroom. After long usage "myth" is still not quite respectable in religious education; it carries too many echoes of fantasy, falsehood and phoniness for some groups. "Ritual," too, may carry unfortunate notions of boring routine, so it may be necessary to use other words, "celebration," "rite," "happening"—whatever serves to help the process of communication. "Structure" and "anti-structure" are Turner's words and even he is sometimes inconsistent in their use. It will probably be counterproductive to use them in some religious education situations. Perhaps the grid and wavy line ciphers of Chapter Five will serve as simple translations of the Turner concepts.

Second, the check-list of recommendations:

1. Use ritual in religious education. Plan for its inclusion in religious education programs.

2. Develop both nonliturgical and liturgical rituals.

3. Begin with the meaning of a ritual:
   Is the emphasis in this ritual to be on structure or anti-structure?
   If the latter, which type of anti-structure will be stressed?

4. Make sure to involve participants in planning the ritual, particularly if communitas is to be stressed.

5. Choose symbols which help express the meaning of the ritual. Where possible make them simple and strong in their appeal to the senses.

6. Make the ritual desirable: the participants should feel that the ritual was worth celebrating. It must not be boring.

7. Involve the participants in ritual. Cut passive spectators to a minimum.

Recommended Reading

1. For Victor Turner's structure/anti-structure theory, start with Chapters 3-5 of his *The Ritual Process*, Cornell University Press, Ithaca, 1969.
   There are also relevant chapters in his *The Forest of Symbols*, Cornell University Press, Ithaca, 1969.

2. For a treatment of liturgy and the sacraments try Lee, B.J. (ed.), *Alternative Futures for Worship*, 7 (small) volumes, The Liturgical Press, Collegeville, Minnesota, 1987.

3. For works exploring the nature of religious education and its links with the imagination, the following are useful:

   Durka, G. and Smith, J., *Aesthetic Dimension of Religious Education*, Paulist, New York, 1979.

   Harris, M., *Teaching and Religious Education*, Harper and Row, San Francisco, 1987.

   Moran, G., *Religious Education as a Second Language*, R.E.P., Birmingham, Alabama, 1989.

   For another approach to religious education, try:

   Grimmitt, M., *Religious Education and Human Development*, McCrimmon, London, 1987.

   Read, G., Rudge, J. and Howarth, R., *How Do I Teach R.E.?* Mary Glasgow, London, (Stanley Thornes, Cheltenham), 1986.

4. Bernstein, E. (ed.), *Liturgy and Spirituality in Context*, The Liturgical Press, Collegeville, Minnesota, 1990. This book contains useful chapters on liturgy, ritual, religious education and the interactions among all three to develop a person's spirituality.

INDEX

aging, 46–7.
alcohol, 49.
Alternative Futures for Worship, 3.
Anointing of the Sick, 105.
anthropology (cultural), 4, 5, 25, 41–2, 111.
anti-structure, 44, 47–66, 67, 73, 74, 83, 111.
   types of anti-structure:
      dangerous, 48–9.
      liminoid, 54–5.
      playful, 49–54.
      relational, 55–9, 74.
      religious, 60–2, 74, 78, 83, 107.
   in the Christian tradition, 62–6.

Baptism, 25, 26–7, 61, 102, 103, 107.
barbeque, 7–10, 13.
Bocock, R., 17, 21.

Callaghan, E., 20–1, 22.
camps, 74–5, 79, 82–4, 89, 92.
Chihamba, 50, 62.
communitas, 55–60, 74, 82, 83, 92, 105, 106, 109, 112.
Confirmation, 25, 60, 105.
Corcoran, K., 36–7.
Cress, F., 28.

desert, 28.
Douglas, M., 48, 106.

Durka, G., *vi*.
Durkheim, E., 25.
Dylan, Bob, 28.

Elias, 57, 59.
Eucharist, 25, 34, 61, 73, 105–9.

folk religion, 50.
Francis of Assisi, 56, 57, 59, 67.
Franciscans, 48, 59.

Gelineau, J., 73.
Geoghegan, Th., 65.
Goldilocks (and the Three Bears), 7, 19.
Green, P., 79, 80.
Guardini, R., 34.
Guzie, T., 3.

Hahn, F., 63–4, 65.
Hay, D., 89.
Hill, N., 27.
Hine, V., 96, 97, 100–1.
Hippolytus, 65.
Hollingworth, P., 108.
Horsley, M., 60–2.
Hutton, D., 27.
Hutton, D.J.R., 27.

Idea of the Holy, The, 87.

Jungmann, J., 64.
Justin, 65.

Kelly, J., 97–8.

King, P., 22.
Kurds, 48, 60.

Lambert, M., 57.
Lanceley, C., 17.
Latvia, 18.
Lee, B., 3.
Leslie, Ch., 60.
liminal(ity), 45, 48, 54, 61, 89.
liminoid, 54–5.
liturgy, 4, 28, 34, 35, 38, 51, 52,
    93, 94, 102, 103–9.
Lonergan, B., 62.

marriage, 13, 24, 46.
Mass, 25, 73, 107.
mateship, 8, 9.
Merton, Th., 28.
Mitchell, N., 3.
Moran, G. 90, 91.
Moss, D., 85, 86.
Moss, P., 84, 85, 86.
mudyi (tree), 43, 44, 48.
Mullins, N., 75, 79.
Mullins, S.,75, 76, 77, 78.
myth, 6, 7, 8, 33, 111.

Ndembu, 22, 42, 48, 50, 54
N'kanga, 42–4, 48.
numinous, 87–8, 89.

Otto, R., 87–8, 89, 91.

"pay-back" system, 11.

Quest for Life, 22.

Rahner, K., 63.
R.C.I.A., 103, 107.

Reconciliation 61, 78, 94–6.
RERU, 89.
revelation, 90.
rings, 23.
rites of passage 42, 68.
Rites of Passage, The, 42.
ritual 3–5, 6, 7, 8, 10, 11, 12, 13,
    17, 18, 19, 20, 23, 25, 26, 29,
    109, 111.
    and action, 33.
    analysis of, 12, 13.
    approaches to, 3.
    as routine, 41.
    complexity of, 17.
    elements of, 17–18.
    importance of, 5.
    liturgical, 103–9.
    non-liturgical, 93–103.
    self-generated, 97, 99–101
    wholeness of, 17.
rituals
    Advent, 84–6.
    AIDS illness, 20–1.
    Child's grief, 79–82.
    Christmas, 51–3.
    Daughter reaching
        maturity, 12.
    Dealing with fears, 97–9.
    Easter, 75–8.
    Farewell to Annie, 101–2.
    Farewell to teacher, 36–7.
    First day at school, 12.
    Prayer group, 100.
    Pre Confirmation, 60–2
    Reconciliation, 94–6.
    Women's ritual, 53–4
Robin Hood, 10.
Robinson, E., 89.
Ryan, T., 27, 52.

sacraments, 3, 4, 26, 105.
Shea, J., 58, 90, 93.
society (and ritual), 4, 5.
Spannagle, P., 94.
structure, 41, 44, 45–7, 57, 65,
    66–7, 68, 73, 82, 83, 99, 103,
    105, 111.
symbol, 18–25, 26, 27, 28, 29,
    94, 108, 109, 112.
  and sign, 18.
  derivation (Greek), 22.
  dominant, 23, 25, 26, 29, 101.
  multivalence of, 22.
  parallels(Desana), 22.
    (Ndembu), 22.
  poles of, 23–4, 29.

private, 19–20, 29.
public,19–20, 21, 29.

Taoist sage, 10.
Turner, V., 3, 23, 25, 29, 42, 44,
    47, 73, 74, 106, 111.

Van Gennep, A., 42, 43.

Webb-Mitchell, B., 41.
Wittgenstein, L., 17.
Worgul, G., 107.
Worship, 3.

Zimbabwe, 26.
Zimmerman, B., 53, 54, 58.